WALSINGHAM

A Year of Celebration

19th August 1997 - 13th September 1998

Commemorating

100 YEARS OF PILGRIMAGE

1897 - 1997

Compiled

by

Timothy V McDonald

Published by R. C. National Shrine, Walsingham.

First published in 1999 by the R. C. National Shrine,
Pilgrim Bureau, Friday Market,
Walsingham, Norfolk, NR22 6EG.

ISBN 0 9502167 7 1

Printed by
The Lanceni Press Ltd, Fakenham, Norfolk.

A Walsingham Centenary Publication

1. Walsingham 100 Years of Pilgrimage 1897 - 1997
    (R. C. National Shrine, 1997)

2. Walsingham England's Nazareth by Peter Rollings
    (R. C. National Shrine, 1998)

3. Walsingham: Methodism in the 19th Century by John Hawkes
    (R. C. National Shrine, 1998)

4. Walsingham: Charlotte Boyd 1837 - 1906 by Kate Moore
    (R. C. National Shrine, 1998)

5. Walsingham: Pilgrimage and History.
    (R. C. National Shrine, 1999)

6   Walsingham: A Year of Celebration.
    (R. C. National Shrine, 1999)

COVER ILLUSTRATIONS:
Front: The Slipper Chapel during the Festival of Flowers.
Back: The Centenary Logo and the Resurrection Station at Sunset.

To

All Pilgrims and Visitors
of all faiths and none
who have travelled to
The Shrine of Our Lady of Walsingham
over the centuries
and especially during
our Centenary Celebrations

CONTENTS

CENTENARY PATRONS

H. E. Cardinal Basil Hume OSB, MA, STL,
Archbishop of Westminster.

Rt. Rev. Peter Smith LLB, JCD,
Bishop of East Anglia.

Rt. Rev. Patrick Leo McCartie,
Bishop of Northampton.

Rt. Rev. Dom Charles Fitzgerald-Lombard OSB, M.Phil,
Former Abbot of Downside,
Titular Abbot of Glastonbury.

Mgr. Anthony G. Stark, KHS,
Master of the Guild of Our Lady of Ransom.

His Grace the Duke of Norfolk,
Maj.-Gen. Sir Miles Fitzalan Howard, KG, GCVO, CB, CBE, MC.

Miss José Noblet,
Chairman of the Walsingham Association.

Foreword

The Centenary of the return of Roman Catholic pilgrimages to Walsingham was marked by more than a year of Celebrations following the opening pilgrimage led by Cardinal Cahal Daly and Bishop Peter Smith on the 20th August 1997. Our celebrations ended with the Dowry of Mary pilgrimage led by Cardinal Basil Hume on 13th September 1998. Between these two dates the National Shrine welcomed many pilgrim groups both new and old; a wonderful programme of concerts and other special events made for a memorable year in the history of the Shrine.

Tim McDonald was the official Centenary Co-ordinator for the Celebrations and must take much of the credit for their great success; wonderful memories of a superb year will be a lasting testament to his hard work. Nigel Kerry proved to be an excellent and unflappable Festival Director and gave us a rich menu of music and song delivered by internationally acclaimed performers and musicians.

I am delighted to welcome this Commemorative Book compiled by Tim McDonald. It will bring back happy memories for those who were present during our Celebrations and also something of the remarkable flavour of things for those who look on from afar.

Father Alan Williams, sm
Director of the National Shrine.

The Book of The Gospels in Procession.
The Walks, King's Lynn, Tuesday 19th August 1997.

THE TIMES
SATURDAY AUGUST 16th 1997

Pilgrims celebrate rebirth of the Shrines
-
Norfolk: While Walsingham welcomes thousands of worshippers, other towns snooze in idyllic anonymity
. -

By TONY KELLY
-

On Wednesday, in a small Norfolk village, Cardinal Cahal Daly, the [former] Roman Catholic Primate of All Ireland, will launch a year of celebrations to commemorate an event that took place 100 years ago this week: the first modern pilgrimage to Walsingham, when 50 Catholic pilgrims arrived on the 12.08 train from King's Lynn. They may not have known it at the time, but those pilgrims were the start of something big. A century on, Walsingham is again a centre of pilgrimage with Anglican and Catholic Shrines attracting half a million pilgrims a year.

It all began in 1061 when the Lady of the Manor, Richeldis de Favarches, had a vision of Our Lady in which she was led to Nazareth to see the "Holy House", where the [arch]Angel Gabriel had appeared. Mary commanded Richeldis to build a replica in Walsingham, and the simple wooden house soon became a place of pilgrimage.

Augustinian and Franciscan monasteries grew up around the site; their remains can still be seen.

By the Middle Ages Walsingham had become the most important Marian Shrine in Christendom.

Henry III made the pilgrimage at least 11 times and gave an annual offering of 40 shillings to the monks. Monarchs up to and including Henry VIII would arrive on horseback and leave their shoes at the 14th century Slipper Chapel and walk the final "holy mile" into Walsingham barefoot.

It was Henry VIII, however who was responsible for Walsingham's decline, when he dissolved the monasteries and had the sub-prior of the abbey [sic] hanged. The Holy House was destroyed in 1538 and the Slipper Chapel became a barn. Henry relented on his deathbed, bequeathing his soul to Our Lady of Walsingham, but the damage had been done.

More than 300 years after the reformation, the idea of pilgrimage was reborn, and the first organised group arrived on August 20th, 1897. Each of the original pilgrims was granted an Indulgence of 40 days by the Bishop of Northampton. Others quickly followed. By the 1930s, the restored Slipper Chapel had become the national Catholic Shrine, and Anglicans - inspired by the Catholic revival of the Oxford Movement - had joined in with a shrine of their own. The Holy House was recreated, this time in brick and stone, and a church built to house it close to the ruined priory...........

The centenary year will see more pilgrims than ever, as the Catholic Pilgrim Bureau lays on a year long festival of music and drama, beginning on September 12th with a concert of Marian music and ending a year later with a performance by the Westminster Cathedral Choir.

The Anglican National Pilgrimage takes place over the 1998 Spring Bank Holiday on May 25th. But though the different churches organise their own events, Walsingham is an ecumenical place, where every pilgrimage features people of all faiths, and none.

My favourite time to visit Walsingham is in winter, when the pilgrims have departed, the souvenir shops are closed and the chapels become places of solitude. As winter turns to spring, the Abbey Gardens are carpeted with snowdrops and this celebration of new life, appearing like magic on the site of Richeldis's Shrine, adds an extra dimension to the visit.

Go this week to share in the centenary celebrations; but if you really want to appreciate Walsingham, go back alone in the winter months and let it speak to you in the silence.

The Replica Statue at The Walks, Tuesday 19th August 1997.

Civic and Ecumenical Guests at The Walks, Tuesday 19th August 1997.

11

The Guardians of the Anglican Shrine at the Walsingham Opening Mass of the Centenary, Wednesday 20th August 1997.

The Guardians in Procession to the Abbey, Wednesday 20th August 1997.

DAILY TELEGRAPH
MONDAY AUGUST 18th 1997

Catholic gesture promotes unity

-

By VICTORIA COMBE, Religion Correspondent

-

Anglicans, for the first time have been invited to join a Roman Catholic procession to mark the centenary of the Shrine of Our Lady of Walsingham in Norfolk. The gesture signals closer relations between the Churches, which both have a shrine at Walsingham, side by side [sic].

Until the late Twenties Catholics would not allow the Anglicans even to step inside their Slipper Chapel and a joint procession would have been unthinkable.

In recognition of this progress the Pope has sent a message supporting the ecumenical nature of the celebrations, saying that the shrine is "fostering new zeal for the restoration of Christian Unity".

At least 15 of the 20 in the College of Guardians of the Anglican Shrine will process on Wednesday afternoon behind Cardinal Cahal Daly the former Primate of All Ireland, from the Slipper Chapel to the Abbey Grounds.......

.........Fr Christopher Colven, former rector of St Stephen's Kensington Road, resigned as Master of the College of Guardians last year when he decided to become a Catholic priest. He has remained a priest guardian.

The trauma of the changes has brought the Catholic and Anglican shrines closer in recent years. The Catholics have invited Barbara Marlow, the first woman guardian, who was appointed in March, to process.

The Anglicans will wear badges of honour and navy velvet cloaks to the dedication service for a new stained glass window in the Slipper Chapel and to Benediction and prayers at the site of the pre-Reformation shrine.

Mrs Marlow, 60, a retired head teacher, said yesterday that she was "thrilled" to be taking part. "Walsingham is all about being ecumenical. We want unity and reconciliation and we are getting there slowly. You cannot rush these things."

EASTERN DAILY PRESS
TUESDAY AUGUST 19th 1997

The Way of the Cross

-

Today is the start of a year long celebration in Walsingham marking the centenary of the restoration of the shrine as a place of pilgrimage.

-

PATRICK BYRNE reports

-

Today's story of Walsingham begins in the mid-19th century and owes a great deal to the Oxford Movement of religious revival and a growing fervour at all levels of society across Europe. The visions of Bernadette Soubirous in Lourdes in the south of France first came to the attention of the local church in 1858. In 1878 Mary Byrne reported the first visions at Knock in the west of Ireland.

In 1897 the first steps to revive the shrine at Walsingham began, and in 1917 a group of children said they had seen an apparition at Fatima in Portugal. During this period, shrines to Mary across Europe took on a new lease of life.

The evidence of this devotional movement is obvious today but it is important to put the story into context.

When the parish priest at King's Lynn, Fr. George Wrigglesworth discovered that his church was on the point of collapse he contacted Fr. Philip Fletcher of the Catholic Church Extension Society which had funds to help.

As they discussed ways of solving the practical problem of saving the fabric of the church they laid the foundations of what is today both devotion and religious tourism. The two priests became great friends and decided to work together to restore Walsingham as a place of pilgrimage.

They obtained permission to refound the shrine from Pope Leo XIII, who also commissioned a statue based on an ancient image of Our Lady in the Church of Santa Maria [in Cosmedin] in Rome.

A replica of the Lady Richeldis' Holy House was built at the church of the Annunciation in King's Lynn.

The Restored Holy House in King's Lynn.

The Restored Replica Statue.

Events were focused on the arrival of the new statue at King's Lynn on August 19th, [1897] and 100 years to the day after its delivery at the main railway station this is remembered.

Anglicans were joining the Roman Church at the time, and among the most devout of these was Charlotte Boyd, who founded and ran an orphanage in Kilburn. She was travelling in Norfolk looking for a house for a group of nuns. She came across the Church of St. Catherine at Houghton-in-the-Dale, which was known as the Slipper Chapel, the last station on the pilgrim road to Walsingham. She bought the chapel, which had been used as a workhouse and a barn, and restored it.

When she was received into the Roman Catholic Church she handed over the chapel to the monks of Downside who were active in Norfolk. This did much to restore Walsingham as a place of pilgrimage.

In the early 1920s, the Anglican vicar of Walsingham erected a statue in the parish church and devotion grew until a shrine was built in 1931.

In 1934 Cardinal Bourne of Westminster and Bishop Youens of Northampton led the first post-Reformation national Pilgrimage to Walsingham and 12,000 people congregated in the fields around the Slipper Chapel.

The post-war years saw a huge growth in the number of pilgrim visitors to Walsingham and in 1948, 14 heavy crosses were carried to the shrine from every part of England as a prayer for peace. These crosses are now a feature of the Roman Catholic Shrine.

Today hundreds of thousands of people visit Walsingham every year and both the Roman Catholic and Anglican Shrines are on their itinerary.

HISTORY

A year long celebration begins at the religious shrine of Walsingham today but the opening venue is King's Lynn. Roman Catholics and Anglicans together are celebrating the anniversary of the restoration of the Walsingham Shrine as a place of pilgrimage to the Virgin Mary 100 years ago.

King's Lynn is the venue because Walsingham was in its Roman Catholic parish boundary 100 years ago when followers of this faith were far fewer than today.

The original shrine, inspired by the Lady Richeldis de Faverches in 1061, was destroyed on the orders of Henry VIII in 1538.

For hundreds of years the wooden replica Holy House of Nazareth and a statue of the Virgin had been places and symbols of a deep devotion. The statue was burned at Chelsea. and the Augustinian Priory whose work had been the care of pilgrims was emptied.

Cardinal Daly will dedicate a restored Holy House and shrine in the Church of the Annunciation, King's Lynn today. Afterwards, there will be a procession to the shrine at Walsingham carrying a replica of the statue of Our Lady which inspired 100 years ago, a renewal of devotion.

EVENTS

Walsingham's Centenary celebrations will last a whole year and the shrine is expecting to enjoy a bumper year with visitors from all across the U.K. and further afield. The year begins with two days of celebration - today and tomorrow.

TODAY [Tuesday 19th August 1997]:

Cardinal Cahal Daly former Archbishop of Armagh and Primate of All Ireland will re-dedicate the restored Holy House and Shrine of Our Lady of Walsingham in the Church of the Annunciation, King's Lynn.

He will also bless the King's Lynn statue and the Walsingham Replica.

The replica statue will be taken in procession to The Walks where, at 11.45 a.m., Bishop Peter Smith of East Anglia will celebrate Mass, as the opening event of the centenary celebrations.......

....After the Solemn Mass, the Guild of Our Lady of Ransom Walkers will process with the replica statue to Massingham St. Mary, a retreat house and convent of the Daughters of Jesus, half way between King's Lynn and Walsingham, where there will be a short service of welcome.

The Red Mount Chapel, The Walks, King's Lynn.

The altar beside the Red Mount Chapel, The Walks, King's Lynn.

19

*Bishop Peter Smith with Councillor Walters and Cardinal Daly, The Red Mount Chapel,
Tuesday 19th August 1997.*

TOMORROW [Wednesday 20th August 1997]:

The replica statue will arrive in time for a Solemn Mass of welcome celebrated by Cardinal Daly at noon. Once again there will be many representatives of national and local organizations at the celebration.

After lunch the Cardinal will unveil the new west window of the Slipper Chapel which depicts the Annunciation and is the work of stained glass artist Alfred Fisher. The Guild of Ransom has donated the window and paid for the restoration of the Slipper Chapel east window, the two statues and the King's Lynn Holy House.

After the window has been blessed, the statue will continue its journey and there will be a procession to the "Abbey" grounds for Benediction. The statue will rest at the original shrine site before being carried the last few yards back along the High Street to its home in the Church of the Annunciation in Friday Market.

There will be a party in the evening in one of the large tents used for the New Dawn Conference. Members of the Norwich Students Jazz Orchestra will provide music, there will be refreshments and a fireworks display designed by the company who staged events to mark VJ day celebrations on the Thames in 1995. There will also be an organ recital in St. Mary's Church.......

Members of the Norwich Students Jazz Orchestra, Wednesday 20th August 1997.

21

DAILY TELEGRAPH
WEDNESDAY AUGUST 20th 1997

Catholics celebrate Centenary of Shrine

-

By VICTORIA COMBE, Religion Correspondent

-

A stained glass window of the Annunciation will be unveiled today in the Roman Catholic Shrine of Our Lady of Walsingham, Norfolk, to mark the centenary of the shrine's restoration.

The ancient shrine of Walsingham was destroyed in 1538, during the Reformation and its statue of Our Lady burned in Chelsea, London. It was refounded in 1897 when Pope Leo XIII sent a statue from Rome to King's Lynn.

The celebrations began yesterday as the statue was carried from the rail station at King's Lynn by members of the Guild of Our Lady of Ransom to the Catholic Church of the Annunciation, King's Lynn.

An outdoor Solemn Mass for 700 was celebrated in the Walks park.

The stained glass window is a gift from the Guild of Our Lady of Ransom, an association dedicated to the conversion of England and Wales, which helped refound the shrine in 1897.

The colourful but otherwise traditional design, by Alfred Fisher, represents the Virgin Mary as a dark-haired Palestinian girl rather than as a fair European girl. Above her are the moon and stars reflecting her position as "Queen of Heaven."

The Catholic Bishop of East Anglia, the Rt. Rev. Peter Smith, and Cardinal Cahal Daly, the former Archbishop of Armagh, are leading the centenary celebrations, which will continue today in Walsingham, the national shrine of Our Lady for Catholics since 1934.

A replica of Pope Leo XIII's statue will be taken to the Slipper Chapel at Houghton St. Giles for a Mass of Welcome celebrated by the Cardinal.

Monsignor Anthony Stark, Master of the Guild of Our Lady of Ransom, with the Leo XIII Statue, arriving at King's Lynn Station, Tuesday 19th August 1997.

The Abbey Arch, Walsingham, during Benediction, Wednesday 20th August 1997.

In a gesture of unity, the College of Guardians from the Anglican shrine at Walsingham have been invited to a blessing service for the new window. They will then proceed, dressed in navy velvet robes to the Abbey grounds for Benediction.

Cardinal Basil Hume, leader of the Roman Catholic Church in England and Wales, sent a message to the shrine commending its "special place in the life of the Church"

"More and more, people are making their way to this, England's Nazareth," he said.

The Congregation at the Centenary Opening Mass, Walsingham, Wednesday 20th August 1997.

EASTERN DAILY PRESS
WEDNESDAY AUGUST 20th 1997

A testament of their faith
-
By RICHARD PARR
-

Celebrations marking the centenary of the re-establishment of pilgrimages to Walsingham began in West Norfolk yesterday when 1,000 people attended an open-air Solemn Mass.

The Red Mount Chapel at King's Lynn, where for centuries pilgrims rested on their way to Walsingham, provided the backdrop for the service attended by Cardinal Cahal Daly, former Primate of All Ireland. People from all over the country attended.

They heard the Roman Catholic Bishop of East Anglia, the Rt. Rev. Peter Smith, speak of the importance of Walsingham as a place of pilgrimage in the approach to the millennium.

Walsingham kept alive the memory of pilgrims, who down the centuries had travelled from all over the world in a spirit of faith, prayer and thanksgiving, he said. "Walsingham stands as a perpetual reminder to the members of each generation of pilgrims that this faith is not merely their own personal possession but that they are inheritors of a tradition of faith handed down to them from the time of the Apostles and the infant Church."

The high altar was on a specially-constructed dais under a canopy in a natural amphitheatre nestling beside the medieval chapel. Taking centre stage was a restored statue of Our Lady.

Before the Mass, the statue was rededicated by Cardinal Daly in a simple ceremony at the town's London Road Roman Catholic Church. It was carried to The Walks by members of the Guild of Our Lady of Ransom.

The Mayor and Mayoress of Lynn, Clifford and Sybil Walters, and the mace-bearers in full regalia added to the colour of the occasion. The full sung Mass and hymns were played over speakers so that the public could join in.

Councillor Clifford Walters, Mayor of the Borough of King's Lynn and West Norfolk in Procession, The Walks, King's Lynn.

The Civic Procession and Fr. Anthony Shryane, R. C. Parish Priest of King's Lynn.

The Guild of Ransom Walkers with the Master of the Guild and the Replica Statue.

The Restored Pope Leo XIII Statue and the Replica Statue in the Church of the Annunciation, King's Lynn.

\-

Sunshine splendour for unique day

\-

Special Report by MICK NOLAN

\-

A special message from the Pope for the people of Lynn was read on Tuesday at a unique ecclesiastical celebration in the town.

Over 1,000 pilgrims basked in glorious sunshine as eminent Roman Catholic clergymen, the most notable being Cardinal Cahal Daly, the former Primate of All Ireland, marked the 100th anniversary of the shrine at Walsingham with a celebration Mass in The Walks.

The National Shrine was refounded in the church of Our Lady of the Annunciation in London Road, hence the reason for Lynn being chosen for such an occasion.

And what an occasion it was. It was one of the most colourful displays to be seen in the town for many years, with countless dignitaries, of all Christian faiths, attending what was a unique day in the history of the town.

STATUE BLESSED

Before the event a replica statue arrived in Lynn by train, just as it had a century ago. Cardinal Daly and the Roman Catholic Bishop of East Anglia, the Rt. Rev. Peter Smith, then attended the Church of the Annunciation, where Cardinal Daly presided over a short ceremony in which the statue was blessed. They then made their way to The Walks for the commemorative Mass which was celebrated by the Bishop.

In the opening sentence of his sermon he said: "If we had been alive one hundred years ago, on August 20 1897, and if we had opened a copy of the Lynn Advertiser we would have read this item. "At Lynn, on Thursday there was a Roman Catholic Pilgrimage to the shrine of Our Lady of Walsingham, in the church here, upon the occasion of the pilgrimage to the shrine of the Blessed Virgin."

With temperatures well into the 80s many of The Walks congregation looked for shade from the baking sun as it beat down relentlessly.

A special altar had been built for the day at the top of steps which lead from the grassy mound at the base of the Red Mount. Special tents were also put up for the visiting clergy and a 30 strong choir.

The Bishop in his sermon gave a brief history of Walsingham and the relevance Lynn has in the Walsingham story. He read the copy of the Lynn News from August 20th 1897, which said : "Under the special sanction and blessing of the Pope, His Holiness Leo XIII, the shrine has been restored by Fr. Wrigglesworth, of Lynn, in the new Roman Catholic church in London Road, Walsingham being in Fr. Wrigglesworth's parish......As Henry VIII utterly destroyed the image, leaving not a vestige remaining, a new image has been especially designated by the Pope on the application of Fr. Wrigglesworth... High Mass over, a procession, including the school children in white, wended its way to the railway station, going through parts of The Walks, which were entered from London Road...The processionists then returned to the church by the same route, with the exception that a detour was made as to include in the route the Chapel of Our Lady on the Mount."

CENTRE OF DEVOTION

Before the end of the ceremony the message from Pope John Paul II was read. It said: "From the time of its establishment in 1061 during the reign of King Saint Edward the Confessor and throughout the middle-ages, the Shrine of Our Lady of Walsingham received pilgrims from throughout Britain and all over Europe, until in 1538, it was tragically destroyed."

He added after more than 350 years it once again became a centre of devotion for pilgrims. "His Holiness prays that those pilgrims will be renewed in faith, love and hope." He finished: "As a sign of his special affection he cordially imparts the requested apostolic blessing."

After the service the Bishop thanked all those who had helped in a celebration which he described as: "going very smoothly."

The Bishop, Cardinal Daly and the Borough Mayor, Clifford Walters, then entered the Chapel of Our Lady on the Mount before the crowds dispersed and the statue continued its journey to Walsingham.

The Centenary Choir.

The Replica Statue leaving The Walks for Massingham St. Mary.

31

Bishop Peter Smith preaching during the Opening Mass of the Centenary, The Walks, King's Lynn, Tuesday 19th August 1997.

HOMILY PREACHED BY
THE RT. REV. PETER SMITH, LLB, JCD,
BISHOP OF EAST ANGLIA.
TUESDAY 19th AUGUST 1997

At the Red Mount Chapel, The Walks, King's Lynn, on the occasion of the Centenary of the Restoration of the Shrine of Our Lady of Walsingham in the Lady Chapel of the Church of the Annunciation, King's Lynn.

If we had been alive one hundred years ago, on August 20th 1897, and if we had opened a copy of the "King's Lynn Advertiser" we would have read this news item:

> "At Lynn, on Thursday, there was a Roman Catholic Pilgrimage to the shrine of Our Lady of Walsingham, in the church, here, upon the occasion of the restoration of the pilgrimage to the shrine of the Blessed Virgin. As part of the church at Lynn, there has been erected a replica of the shrine formerly existing at Walsingham... In the Middle Ages the shrine at Walsingham was the most famous one in Christendom, pilgrimages being made to it from far and near, and its fame may be gathered from the fact that among the worshippers were the Plantagenet Kings of England, including King Henry VIII, (by whose orders some time afterwards the statue was burnt at Chelsea)."

Or, the next day, we might have read in the "Lynn News" a slightly different account which included these details:

> "Under the special sanction and blessing of the Pope, His Holiness Leo XIII, the shrine has been restored by Fr. Wrigglesworth, of Lynn, in the new Roman Catholic church in London Road, Walsingham being in Fr. Wrigglesworth's parish... As Henry VIII utterly destroyed the image, leaving not a vestige remaining, a new image has been specially designated by the Pope on the application of Fr Wrigglesworth... High Mass over, a procession, including the school children in white (with blue sashes), wended its way to the railway station, going through parts of the Walks, which were entered from London Road... The processionists then returned to

the church by the same route, with the exception that a detour was made so as to include in the route the Chapel of Our Lady on the Mount."

So began, 100 years ago, the refounding and renewal of the medieval shrine of Our Lady of Walsingham. The day after the celebrations in King's Lynn, Fr. Wrigglesworth and Fr. Fletcher, the Master of the Guild of Our Lady of Ransom, led the first Guild pilgrimage to Walsingham on August 20th 1897 - the very first since the Reformation and the suppression of the Shrine at Walsingham in August 1538. Those Guild pilgrimages continued each year for the next thirty-five years, until on August 15th 1934, the then Bishop of Northampton, Bishop Laurence Youens, re-opened the Slipper Chapel at Walsingham by celebrating Mass there for the first time since the Reformation. This was to prepare for the first National Pilgrimage to Walsingham, led by Cardinal Francis Bourne on August 19th 1934, and the formal translation of the Shrine from King's Lynn back to Walsingham itself.

However, in 1921 a new era in Walsingham's history had already begun, when Alfred Hope Patten became the new vicar of St. Mary's Anglican Church in Walsingham. In the Anglo-Catholic tradition of the Church of England, Alfred Hope Patten was a man of great energy and enthusiasm who very much wanted to restore an ancient shrine of Our Lady in England. And so he did, first of all in St. Mary's, and then following the purchase of land nearby, by building a replica of the original 'holy house' in a special shrine church independent of the parish, which was begun in 1931 and has developed extraordinarily over the intervening years. How astonished the clergy and people of that time would have been, to know how wonderfully and fruitfully ecumenical relationships have developed and flourished in the second half of this century under the prompting and guidance of the Holy Spirit! That is something for which we should all thank God for today.

But as we know, the origins of the Shrine of Our Lady of Walsingham lie much further back in history. Founded in the eleventh century as a replica of the holy house of Nazareth, it was dedicated to the mystery of the Annunciation and over the years began to attract an ever increasing number of pilgrims both from home and abroad. With its growth in prominence, the Bishop of Norwich entrusted the care of the shrine to the Augustinian Canons in 1153, who built a monastery there with a new Priory church which was magnificently rebuilt in 1401. For nearly 500 hundred years Walsingham attracted great numbers of ordinary pilgrims, as well as at least nine Kings of England from Richard I to Henry VIII, and eminent scholars such as Erasmus, until its dissolution in 1538.

What then, constitutes the uniqueness of Walsingham, and what is its significance as a Marian Shrine? Walsingham is unique in so far as it is about a place, rather than a picture or statue. As Monsignor Anthony Stark, the present Master of the Guild of Our Lady of Ransom reminds us in his note on the historical background to the Shrine:

> "Although there are a number of Marian shrines which predate Walsingham, these are usually centred around a statue or a picture with a reputation for miracles. However, because of Our Lady's specific request, Walsingham was unique in that it was the Holy Place itself that was the object of devotion as at Loretto two centuries later and may be regarded as the first International Marian Shrine in the Catholic Church - a veritable 'medieval Lourdes'. Indeed, it ranked as one of the four great shrines of the Middle Ages, with Jerusalem, Rome, and Santiago de Compostella - and uniquely in honour of the Holy Mother of God. With the closure of the Holy Land to most Christian pilgrims, 'England's Nazareth' acquired a special significance."

What is the significance of Walsingham as a place of pilgrimage? What message does Walsingham convey to us as we come to the close of the second Millennium and approach the beginning of the third?

First of all it keeps alive and fresh in our own minds and hearts the memory of all those Christians, with whom we are united as members of the communion of saints, who have come in pilgrimage over the centuries in a spirit of faith, prayer and thanksgiving to God who is our Father. And it keeps alive in our own day the memory of those truths of faith which we share with them still - the faith expressed so succinctly in the ancient Creeds such as the one we will profess together in this Mass today. It is a perpetual reminder to the members of each generation of pilgrims that this faith is not merely their own personal possession, but that they are the inheritors of a tradition of faith which has been handed down to them through the centuries, from the time of the Apostles and the infant Church. It is a reminder too that each generation has a sacred duty to hand on that tradition of faith to future generations in obedience to the command of Our Lord Jesus Christ.

Equally significant, I believe, is that Walsingham is dedicated to the Annunciation. Of that event we read in the first chapter of St. Luke's Gospel:

> "... the angel said to her, 'Mary, do not be afraid; you have won God's favour. Listen! You are to conceive and bear a son, and you must name him Jesus. He will be great and will be called Son of the Most High. The Lord God will give him the throne of his ancestor David; he will rule over the House of Jacob for ever and his reign will have no end.'" (Lk. 1:30-33)

It was through the Annunciation, and through Mary's "yes", that the way was opened for the fulfilment of the Mystery of the Incarnation, the origin and ground of Mary's joy, and indeed of our joy today. With the Annunciation at Nazareth, the final stages of salvation history began to unfold. And it was with the house in Nazareth, with all that it signified, that Walsingham was identified, so the symbolism of the house at Nazareth is important The replica of that house, built at Walsingham, was a place for Christians to come and to stand symbolically, so to speak, where Mary had stood, to say "yes" to God, to whatever he might ask; to come, like Mary, to "listen" and ponder the Word of God and so to become in the deepest sense a hearer of the Word and a bearer of the Holy Spirit.

At the Annunciation, that young virgin in Nazareth gave her wholehearted "yes" to what God asked of her. She was the one chosen by God and asked to give life in this world to him who is the light of the world, and the life of the world. As St. John has it in the Prologue to his Gospel:

> "In the beginning was the Word:
> the Word was with God
> and the Word was God.
> He was with God in the beginning.
> Through him all things came to be,
> not one thing had its being but through him.

All that came to be, had life in him
and that life was the light of men,
a light that shines in the dark,
a light that darkness could not overpower...
The Word was made flesh,
he lived among us,
and we saw his glory,
the glory that is his as the only Son of the Father,
full of grace and truth."

By sending his only-begotten Son into the world, God became one like us in all things but sin and offered us the gift of eternal life. And as Pope John Paul II has reminded us, the

"one who accepted "Life" in the name of all, and for the sake of all, was Mary, the Virgin Mother:.. and Mary's consent at the Annunciation and her motherhood stand at the very beginning of the mystery of life which Christ came to bestow on humanity." (Evangelium Vitae, 102)

So, when we reflect on the mystery of the Incarnation, and the role that the Blessed Virgin was asked to play in it, we are lead

"to a most profound understanding of Mary's experience as the incomparable model of how life should be welcomed and cared for." (ibid.)

Mary brought "Life" into the world; the "Light" who wants only to lead us into the fullness of truth - about God, about the purpose of human life, about what it means to be truly human. This gospel, this good news is for us the ultimate source of our joy and celebration, for the meaning of life is found in giving and receiving unconditional love. It is the good news

"of a living God who is close to us, who calls us to profound communion with himself and awakens in us the certain hope of eternal life... It is the presentation of human life as a life of relationship, a gift of God, the fruit and sign of his love. It is the proclamation that Jesus has a unique relationship with every person, which enables us to see in every human face the face of Christ." (E.V., 81)

To love means to care for the other as a person for whom God has made us responsible. As disciples of Jesus we are called to become neighbours to everyone, and to show special favour to those who are poorest, most alone, and most in need. In helping the hungry, the thirsty, the foreigner, the naked, the sick, the imprisoned - as well as the child in the womb and the old person who is suffering or near death - we have the opportunity to serve Jesus. He himself said:

"As you did it to one of the least of these my brethren, you did it to me." (Mt. 25:40)

This message of life and love is for everybody without exception. It is precisely because of the Incarnation, God becoming man, that we are assured of God's passionate concern for each and every one of us in this life as well as the next. He most certainly asks us to love him as he has first loved us. "You must love the Lord your God with all your heart, and all your strength and all your mind." But he also commands us to love our neighbour as ourselves - and that means that our love must be directed not only to Him, but to each other, to the good of individuals and to the common good of the community, local and global. In this respect, the Holy Father has reminded us once again in his Encyclical Letter, "Evangelium Vitae":

"It is impossible to further the common good without acknowledging and defending the right to life, upon which all the other inalienable rights of individuals are founded and from which they develop. A society lacks solid foundations when, on the one hand, it asserts values such as the dignity of the person, justice and peace, but then, on the other hand, radically acts to the contrary by allowing or tolerating a variety of ways in which human life is devalued and violated, especially where it is weak or marginalised. Only respect for life can be the foundation and guarantee of the most precious and essential goods of society, such as democracy and peace. There can be no true democracy without a recognition of every person's dignity and without respect for his or her rights." (E.V., 101)

The significance of Walsingham for me, is that it is a place in which we are reminded that it was at Nazareth that Mary opened her heart fully to the Holy

Spirit and so opened the way for the Incarnation. It was there that she welcomed and rejoiced in the gift of that life which was given to her to nourish and nurture for the sake of the whole human race. It is a place to which we can come and in which we can renew our own personal "yes" to the gift of life and love which God gives to each and every one of us as a totally unconditional gift. It is a place where we can come to be refreshed, renewed and strengthened through prayer and the sacraments, especially the Eucharist and the Sacrament of Reconciliation. And so, nourished, renewed and refreshed, we can return to our day to day lives and live out that commandment of love, of compassion and of hope, whatever our circumstances and whatever the difficulties we may face. Like Mary, we can be confident that he will accompany us at every step on our journey and we will be guided and guarded at every stage by his providential care. The message of Walsingham, then, is a message of hope, of reassurance and of confidence: "Do not be afraid ... for nothing is impossible to God."

His Eminence Cardinal Cahal Daly, The Walks, King's Lynn, Tuesday 19th August 1997.

The Replica Statue at Houghton St. Giles, Wednesday 20th August 1997.

Crossing the Stiffkey, Wednesday 20th August 1997.

EASTERN DAILY PRESS
THURSDAY AUGUST 21st 1997

Joyous day for Shrine pilgrims

About 1,700 pilgrims gathered at Walsingham yesterday to celebrate a special anniversary in the company of Cardinal Cahal Daly, former Primate of All Ireland.

-

JOHN BULTITUDE
joined the crowds marking the centenary of the Roman Catholic Shrine.

-

As people parked their cars and unpacked the necessities for a day in the sun, the distinctive buzz of a special occasion spread through the crowds. There was a cosmopolitan burr of accents as the Yorkshire roar mingled with the flat Midlands speech and the sing-song Irish lilt.

There was almost a holiday atmosphere as the visitors gathered at Walsingham to mark the centenary of modern pilgrimage to the village. They carried deckchairs, picnic baskets and the obligatory umbrella to keep out the sun's searching rays.

As the build-up continued, the excitement threshold rose and everyone was keen to share in the joy of the occasion. One middle-aged woman abandoned decorum and almost danced with delight as she trilled to a friend: "I have just met the Cardinal."

But the high temperatures were not to everyone's liking. One priest with a face glowing beetroot muttered quietly to himself: "This is not a pilgrimage. This is more of a penance."

The competition for a spot in the shade was fierce but good-humoured. And some were happy to brave the sun's rays for a front row seat at the festivities. Leicester couple Charles and Maud Simms were glad they had made the trip to Norfolk. Mr Simms said that Cardinal Daly had recognised his Irish accent and they had had a chat. As they relaxed and waited for the Solemn Mass of Welcome to begin, the couple, who have a holiday home at nearby Wells had just one disappointment. "I have come here today without my camera," said Mrs Simms.

Then the bells at the Slipper Chapel just outside Walsingham began to toll heralding the arrival of a small group of pilgrims who had walked from Fakenham. They were carrying a replica statue of the one blessed by Pope Leo XIII which marked the return of the Catholic Shrine of Our Lady of Walsingham 100 years ago.

Cardinal Daly, who took the service, said he was privileged to be invited to participate in the start of the Walsingham festivities. He said "I have, of course been to Walsingham, on two previous occasions. One, I have to admit was nearly 50 years ago, and the other was four or five years ago. I felt then, and I feel today, that joy and peace in believing, which is a mark of all Marian Shrines."

He also made a timely plea for the problems in Ireland to be brought to an end. "Although they are not primarily religious, there is a sectarian element contributing to the conflict," he said. Cardinal Daly said that this was a cause of great shame and pain to his fellow countrymen.

Although his words brought comfort and thought to many, it all went over the heads of some of the younger pilgrims. One little girl opted to soil her Sunday best by playing with her pet dog while another tot lay asleep in his cot, an occasional twitching toe the only sign of life.

Then the hundreds of people moved on to the Slipper Chapel to witness Cardinal Daly bless the centenary stained glass window bought by the Guild of Our Lady of Ransom, whose previous members refounded the Shrine of Our Lady of Walsingham a century ago.

The statue was then taken to the site of the pre-reformation shrine in Walsingham Abbey grounds before ending its journey at the Roman Catholic parish Church of the Annunciation in the village's Friday Market.

As the pilgrims returned to their airless cars and prepared for the journey home, the celebrations were far from over. The next 13 months will see the anniversary marked in a number of diverse ways. But yesterday's pilgrims knew they had participated in a special form of worship and had been given a once in a lifetime chance to share their religious joy.

The Priest's Procession, Wednesday 20th August 1997.

Cardinal Daly and Bishop Smith in the Church of the Annunciation,
Wednesday 20th August 1997.

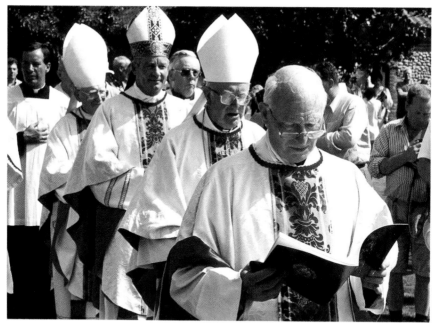

Cardinal Daly, Bishop Smith, Bishop Clark and Mgr. Stark in Procession, Wednesday 20th August 1997.

The Guardians of the Anglican Shrine entering The Abbey Gate after Processing from the Slipper Chapel, Wednesday 20th August 1997.

THE INDEPENDENT
THURSDAY AUGUST 21st 1997

-

Two faiths become one at Norfolk Shrine

-

By LOUISE JURY

-

It was a small gesture bridging the religious divide. Twenty Anglicans marked by their striking blue capes, joined nearly 1,900 Catholics to mark 100 years of pilgrimage to the tiny shrine at Walsingham, Norfolk.

Their presence would have been unheard of in 1897 when 40 Catholics held the first public pilgrimage to the village's Slipper Chapel after a break of 350 years.

As recently as the late 1920s, Anglicans were not even allowed to enter the chapel whose name derives from the pilgrims' habit of leaving their shoes and walking a final further mile to Walsingham's ruined priory on foot.

But yesterday, it was as if the boiling sunshine had brought out a warm spirit of religious tolerance. Fr Martin Warner, the Administrator of a nearby Anglican Shrine, said everything was going "magnificently".

"This says quite clearly that Walsingham is a place of ecumenism," he said. Whatever divisions in doctrine elsewhere, he and his counterpart at the Catholic shrine, Fr Alan Williams, work together often.

Admittedly some of the Guardians of the Anglican shrine have gone one step further - they actually converted to Rome. And other pilgrimages have faced fierce anti-Pope demonstrations. But yesterday Fr Warner insisted: "The experience of coming to Walsingham is one of healing. I think that's what motivates people to come here and I think that's what they discover."

As pilgrims arrived with white cotton hats, picnic hampers, garden chairs and umbrellas as parasols, the celebration had the air of a garden party rather than a religious service. The level of excitement at a sighting of the former Primate of [All] Ireland, Cardinal Cahal Daly, placed him in a minor film star league. He led the open-air Mass, then the procession through the tree lined lanes of Norfolk to finish the pilgrimage.

As in days gone by, some pilgrims walked with bare feet on the scalding tarmac. Others hobbled bravely on sticks or travelled by wheelchair, reciting prayers and clutching rosary beads. A young Irish boy refused his brother a drink from his water bottle. "John Paul, it's only mineral water, let him have it," said his Mother. "No it's not, Ma" he replied. "I filled it up with holy water."

A party from St John Bosco church in Blackley, Manchester, had left home at 6.30 a.m. to get to what is regarded as Nazareth for Britain's Catholics, their most important religious site. Agnes Lewis, 58, a retired teacher, came because she has been recently widowed after caring for her sick husband for some time. "It was just something I felt I wanted to do," she said.

Sheila Pawson, 47, a medical secretary, comes regularly with her diocese. Pauline Millington, 50, also a medical secretary was on her first visit. None had known the Anglicans were invited, though all thought it was a good thing. "I think it's good we're all together," she said. Ms Millington agreed. "Things are changing."

Peter Brogan, 43, a deacon from Lincoln, was on holiday with wife Mary, 37, and three of their children. "I think we've got to be more ecumenical now," he said. "The one important thing that we've got to realise is that we're a Christian country."

The Centenary Procession from the Slipper Chapel in Walsingham, High Street, Wednesday 20th August 1997.

The Replica Statue is welcomed home by Rev. Peter Allen, sm, Walsingham's Roman Catholic Parish Priest, Wednesday 20th August 1997.

His Eminence Cardinal Cahal Daly, Former Primate of All Ireland, preaching at the Centenary Mass, Wednesday 20th August 1997.

48

HOMILY PREACHED BY
HIS EMINENCE CARDINAL CAHAL DALY
FORMER ARCHBISHOP OF ARMAGH AND PRIMATE OF ALL IRELAND
Wednesday 20th August 1997

At the National Shrine of Our Lady on the occasion of the Centenary of the First Post Reformation Pilgrimage to the Slipper Chapel, Walsingham.

I feel privileged to have been invited by the Master of the Guild of Our Lady of Ransom, Monsignor Anthony Stark, and by the Bishop of East Anglia, Right Rev Peter Smith, to take part in the celebrations to mark the Centenary of the first pilgrimage to the Shrine of Our Lady of Walsingham since the Reformation; that first pilgrimage was organised by the Guild in 1897. I have very happy memories of my own first pilgrimage to Walsingham, which the Guild kindly asked me to join a few years ago. I found at Walsingham that "joy and peace in believing" of which Saint Paul speaks, and which is a characteristic of all Marian Shrines; so I had no hesitation in at once accepting the invitation to return in this special Walsingham year.

THE "HOLY HOUSE AT WALSINGHAM"

Walsingham first attracted attention as a shrine of Our Lady when a holy aristocratic lady in the locality was favoured by visions in which she was asked by Our Blessed Mother to erect on her estate a replica of the Holy House of Nazareth, to honour the mystery of the Annunciation. This was in the year 1061, in the reign of Saint Edward the Confessor. Reports of cures soon followed and the reputation of the Walsingham Shrine spread. Crowds began to come to Walsingham on pilgrimage. The Bishop of Norwich entrusted the care of the Shrine to the Augustinian Canons, who built the Romanesque Priory, within whose ruins we complete to-day's celebrations. The Priory Church was enlarged at the beginning of the fifteenth century, with a Lady Chapel built over the original Holy House. Devotions and pilgrimages to honour Our Lady of Walsingham continued for 500 years until the monastery, church and shrine were destroyed under King Henry VIII in 1538. The same King Henry had, earlier in his life, shown a remarkable devotion to Our Lady and had come on pilgrimage several times to Walsingham and enriched the shrine with generous donations.

49

Walsingham in this period became, in fact, if not in name, England's National Shrine of Our Lady. Indeed it came to rank among the great pilgrimage centres of Europe, side by side with Jerusalem, Rome and Compostella. Erasmus, the great Renaissance humanist and scholar, writes of making the pilgrimage twice; and in one letter he says that it is the ambition of every English man and woman to go on pilgrimage to Walsingham at least once in their lifetime, though many go every year.

Nine Kings of England in succession came here, often accompanied by their Queens. The place where we now stand, the route we followed yesterday from King's Lynn to Red Mount Chapel, to Fakenham, to the Slipper Chapel, and the route of our procession this afternoon to the Priory grounds, are sanctified by the prayers of countless pilgrims of the past, who implored the Lord through the intercession of Saint Mary the Virgin to bless England and its Monarch and to keep England in the true path of the salvation brought into our world by the Son of God and Son of Mary in the Holy House of Nazareth 2000 years ago.

PILGRIMAGE IN CHRISTIAN HISTORY

It is good to remember the place which pilgrimage has played in Christian life down the centuries, and the impact which pilgrimage made on our culture, our language and literature, our art and our music. It has often been said that the main motive for building roads throughout history has been the movement of troops for the waging of war or the subjugation of peoples; and this is sadly true. But in the middle ages many of Europe's major roads as well as ports were designed as pilgrim routes; for example, North and South highways leading to Saint James or Santiago de Compostella, or West-East roads leading to Rome and Jerusalem. This was so in England in the case of Canterbury and Walsingham.

Pilgrimages influenced our language of travel; to "saunter" first meant to journey to the Holy Land, the "Saunte Terre"; "to canter" meant to ride to Canterbury like Chaucer's pilgrims; "to roam" meant to go on pilgrimage to Rome, the "Eternal City". Chaucer shows that pilgrimages had their celebratory side as well as their penitential and prayerful side; they were celebrations of human life, as well as of the eternal life revealed to us in Jesus Christ; indeed, celebration of Eternal Life implies also celebration of all that is good and true and beautiful in earthly human life. At a recent conference of the Ecumenical Society of the Blessed Virgin Mary, a leading specialist in the history of music offered us a memorable presentation of a typical medieval pilgrimage to Walsingham, with slides showing the various towns and wayside chapels where pilgrims prayed on their route or rested for the night, and accompanied by music, sacred and secular, played on instruments of the period, original or in the style of the period, as this is illustrated in medieval carvings or paintings. That was indeed "merrie England", Mary's Dowry, celebrating the glories of Mary, England's and mankind's Heavenly Queen.

MODERN WALSINGHAM

The story of modern Walsingham may be said to have begun in 1894, with the purchase of the Slipper Chapel, which by then had been turned into a cottage, by a devout Anglican lady who later became a Catholic. The chapel was the last of the wayside chapels which marked stages on the pilgrim route to Walsingham. It was the Guild of Our Lady of Ransom which took part in the restoration of the Shrine and the pilgrimage. Founded in 1887, the Guild quickly decided to make this restoration one of its first aims. Not a single Catholic lived in the neighbourhood of Walsingham at the time; so it was decided to restore the shrine in the nearest Catholic Church, which was at King's Lynn. A new church was being built in King's Lynn at this time; and the Parish Priest, aided by the Founder of the Guild, Father Philip Fletcher, created a Lady Chapel in his new church, modelled on the Holy House of Loreto, which pious tradition held to be the Holy House of Nazareth itself. Pope Leo XIII blessed the project and personally selected a statue of Our Lady in the Church of Santa Maria in Cosmedin as a model for a new statue of Our Lady of Walsingham, to replace the ancient one, which had been destroyed at the Reformation, and of which no reproduction was then known.

Yesterday, 19th August, in the year 1897, the Guild organised the first pilgrimage to Our Lady of Walsingham in three-and-a-half centuries. The new statue was delivered from Rome that morning and was carried in solemn procession to the new church at King's Lynn and installed there. On the next day, the pilgrims continued to Walsingham and walked, reciting the Rosary, to the Slipper Chapel. The Chapel had not yet been opened for worship, and the pilgrims walked around it, praying, and then walked on to the ruins of the Priory. This set the pattern for all future pilgrimages, and this pattern is being followed exactly in this centenary year, with celebrations beginning in King's Lynn yesterday and culminating today in Walsingham.

The intention from the beginning, however, was to restore the shrine and the pilgrimage to the original location in Walsingham itself. On 19th August 1934, a new Catholic Parish was set up at Fakenham, and at this time Cardinal Bourne transferred the shrine to the Slipper Chapel, while the Pope Leo XIII statue remained at King's Lynn. In 1921, an Anglican Shrine of Our Lady of Walsingham had been established in the village by Rev. Alfred Hope-Patten. He was able to trace from a medieval seal the shape of the pre-Reformation statue of Our Lady of Walsingham; and hence to have a statue made resembling the original; this statue was installed in the Anglican Shrine Church. A new statue, also modelled on this seal, was installed in the Slipper Chapel by Cardinal Bourne on 19th August 1934, and there it still stands.*

I mentioned earlier the Ecumenical Society of the Blessed Virgin Mary. The Society was founded by another great convert, Martin Gillett. It was he who, in 1935, organised the first London to Walsingham walk. The annual Cross-carrying Pilgrimage of fourteen groups converging on Walsingham from fourteen different parts of the country began in 1948. The Guild of Our Lady of Ransom initiated annual Walsingham Walks in 1952; this year sees the Guild's 46th walk. Walsingham featured prominently in England's celebration of the Marian year 1954. In the course of the first National Pilgrimage to Walsingham that year, a huge concourse of pilgrims witnessed the crowning of the statue of Our Lady of Walsingham by Archbishop O'Hara, Apostolic Delegate, in the name of Pope Pius XII. Since 1968, the Marist Fathers have been entrusted with charge of the Shrine, helped in their charge by a group of Marist Sisters. In the 1980s a new shrine church, the Chapel of Reconciliation, was built. The statue of Our Lady of Walsingham was taken to Wembley for the Mass celebrated by the Holy Father during his visit to this country in 1982.

Among today's centenary events is the dedication of a new Annunciation window in the Slipper Chapel, which I am to have the privilege of blessing and unveiling today; it is a gift from the Guild of Our Lady of Ransom. The Guild is also having the Assumption window in the Slipper Chapel restored, and is at the same time undertaking to pay for the restoration of the "Holy House" and of the Leo XIII statue at King's Lynn. The Guild deserves, therefore, gratitude from all of us on this day; but, what is more important for them is that Our Lady must smile at them today affectionately and gratefully, joining with them in glorifying the Lord for all the graces and blessing showered through the powerful prayers of Mary upon all who visit Walsingham and all those for whom they pray.

MARY, VIRGIN MOST POWERFUL

The idea is sometimes put about nowadays that the figure of Mary has been used by the "patriarchal Church" for the oppression of women. Mary has been presented, it is claimed, as timid, submissive, meek, obedient, a model for the subordinate and docile and submissive woman which the "male church" wished all women to be. This is a caricature. Mary has always been presented by the Church as a model for all followers of Jesus, males as well as females. Her obedience is nothing other than an outstanding instance of the obedience to God's Word and Will which is required of every disciple of the Lord. Mary has always been shown to us by the Church as a strong woman, who stood by her Son on Calvary, when all the male disciples except John had fled.

In the most familiar of our litanies, the Litany of Loreto, Mary is invoked as "Mirror of Justice", "Queen of Martyrs", "Tower of David", "Virgin most Powerful", "Help of Christians", "Virgin most Faithful", scarcely the epithets which we use for "timid and submissive" women!

The original medieval statue of Our Lady of Walsingham, on which our present statue is modelled, is typical of the early and medieval representations of Mary. She is shown as a strong mother, with one protecting arm around her Son, the other hand pointing to Him, as though to say to us: "Here is your Lord, here is your God; follow Him; listen to Him; do whatever He tells you". Mary has a gentle but determined look; she looks the world in the eye without fear; she is ready to "take on" the world in vindication of the Divine Rights of her Son. Such too were the most famous icons in the Churches of the East, always showing Mary as the Mother of the King of all Kings, the Mother filled with loving pride in her Son, lovingly and willingly obedient and submissive to Him alone, and asking from all of us, obedient and submissive love for him. Truly, as Pope Paul VI put it, Mary;

> "offers a calm vision and reassuring word to modern men and women." (Marialis Cultus 57)

In the magnificent document on true devotion to the Blessed Virgin Mary from which I have been quoting, Pope Paul VI warned against unhealthy forms of devotion to Our Lady, and particularly against "the exaggerated search for novelties or extraordinary phenomena". Among these unhealthy manifestations of Marian devotion, we must surely name the excessive credulity which is sometimes nowadays shown towards alleged "visions" and "messages", often accompanied by dire warnings of divine punishment and coming doom. Such apocalyptic phenomena seem to increase as we approach a new millennium; they are not the Church's way or the Gospel's way or Mary's way of preparing for the end of the second Millennium. Instead, we must try to enter deeply into the programme of spiritual renewal outlined for us by Pope John Paul II and by the Bishops of each country for this year 1997 and for the two years which follow before the great Jubilee of the Redemption in the year 2000.

CHRISTIAN UNITY

In that programme, an important place is accorded by the Pope to work and prayer for Christian Unity. In this document for the new Millennium, "Tertio Millennio Adveniente," Pope John Paul strikingly calls for repentance for sins against unity committed in the past. Sadly, he says, in the past, and particularly in the second millennium,

> "ecclesial communion has been painfully wounded; and at times people of both sides were to blame."

He goes on

> "such wounds openly contradict the will of Christ and are a cause of scandal to the world" (T.M.A. 44).

The Pope calls for intense and urgent prayer for Christian Unity as part of our preparation for the Great Jubilee.

I referred earlier to the Ecumenical Society of the Blessed Virgin Mary and its founder, Martin Gillett. His vision was of a Society which would bring together Christians of all denominations in a common desire for Christian unity, and he saw Mary, Mother of God, as a focus for unity of love and for sharing of devotion and faith between the participants. At the inaugural meeting of the Birmingham branch in 1971, the then Anglican Bishop of Birmingham, Doctor Laurence Brown, said:

> "If anyone is going to bring the Churches of Christ together, then it would be Mary, the Mother of Christ".

That is our conviction, that is our prayer, as we gather today before Our Lady's Shrine. The Anglican shrine nearby is surely already a harbinger of unity and a source of hope for further progress on the pilgrim road to Christian unity.

Although our tragic conflicts in Northern Ireland are not primarily religious, there is undoubtedly a sectarian element contributing to the conflict. This must be a cause of great pain and shame to us all. I ask for your prayers in this Chapel of Reconciliation that conflict in Northern Ireland may soon be brought to a permanent end, with agreement between all parties in our divided society, and with reconciliation and forgiveness and Christian love marking all relationships within the island of Ireland and relationships between Ireland and Britain, replacing the bitter chapters which have marred past history.

CONVERSION OR ECUMENISM?

The Guild of Our Lady of Ransom was established with as its aim "the conversion of England and Wales". In these post-Council years, this aim is sometimes seen as being in conflict with the Church's commitment to Church unity. Conversion and ecumenism are said to be incompatible. The Vatican Council itself explicitly asserts the opposite. In its Decree on Ecumenism, the council states;

> "It is evident that the work of preparing and reconciling those individuals who wish for full Catholic communion is of its nature distinct from ecumenical action. But there is no opposition between the two, since both proceed from the wondrous providence of God." (Unitatis Redintegratio 2)

It is important to remember, however, that the most important means to the conversion of others is the conversion of ourselves; reconciliation of others with the communion of the Catholic Church requires first of all reconciliation of ourselves with God and with His Church, in full communion of mind and heart with Pope John Paul, centre of unity in the Catholic Church, and with the Bishops whom the Holy Spirit has "appointed as overseers to rule the Church of God". It is above all what Pope John Paul has called the "contagion of holiness" among Catholics which draws others to the Catholic Church. May the fruits of this centenary year of Walsingham be for all of us the grace of true conversion and growth in holiness.

CARDINAL NEWMAN'S PRAYER

On this great occasion my mind goes back to Cardinal Newman's famous sermon on "The Second Spring". It was preached at St. Mary's, Oscott, at the First Provincial Synod of Westminster in July 1852, 45 years before the first post-Reformation pilgrimage to Walsingham. Newman invoked Our Lady;

"It is the time for thy visitation. Arise, Mary, and go forth in thy strength into that North Country, which was once thine own, and take possession of a land which knows thee not. Arise, Mother of God, and with thy thrilling voice, speak to those who labour with child, and are in pain, till the babe of grace leaps within them! Shine on us dear Lady, with thy bright countenance, like the sun in his strength, O Stella Matutina, O Harbinger of Peace, till our year is one perpetual May ..... O Mary, my hope, O Mother undefiled, fulfil to us the promise of this Spring" (Sermons preached on Various Occasions, 1904, p. 177).

Since Newman spoke, the Church in our islands, the Church all over the world, has known great triumphs, but also great setbacks, it has known both joy and hope, grief and anxiety. In our time it is faced with immense opportunities, but also with very grave problems. Once again, let the words of Newman give us confidence and renew our hope, as one century nears its end and a new century and a new millennium are soon to be born:

"Mary's Son will deny her nothing that she asks, and herein lies her power. While Mary defends the Church, neither height nor depth, neither men nor evil spirits, neither great monarchs, nor craft of man, nor popular violence, can avail to harm us; for human life is short, but Mary reigns above, a Queen for ever." (Prayers, Verses and Devotions, Ignatius Press, 1989.)

*This Statue was replaced by the statue blessed and crowned by Archbishop O'Hara in the name of Pope Pius XII, on 15th August 1954.

Cardinal Cahal Daly with Bishop Alan Clark in the Abbey Grounds, Walsingham, Wednesday 20th August 1997.

Installation of the Centenary Window.

CHURCH BUILDING MAGAZINE

ISSUE 47, SEPTEMBER/OCTOBER 1997

-

Walsingham new glass at the Slipper Chapel

-

By ALFRED FISHER

-

For well over 300 years before the Reformation the roads to Walsingham Priory had been well trodden by pilgrims from all parts of the country and overseas. Katherine of Aragon was a regular visitor. Edward I made the pilgrimage on 12 occasions, and even Henry VIII who, years later, was to be responsible for the start of its descent to destruction.

Such pilgrims would stop at chapels en-route but for a particular purpose at St. Catherine's Chapel a mile distant from their destination. There they would remove footwear and painfully walk barefoot for the final mile. This "Slipper Chapel" survives and after varied fortunes over 450 years is now the National Catholic Shrine which welcomes 230,000 modern pilgrims every year to prayer and praise.

Although the tiny chapel is usually recorded as having been re-discovered in the 1890s surrounded by farm buildings, it was measured and sketched by A.W.N. Pugin as early as 1831, when the west front appears much as it does today.

Its elevation to the status of National Shrine, took place only in 1934 but, on August 20th 1897, the first public pilgrimage to Walsingham since the Reformation took place, and to celebrate the centenary of this event this year, it was decided to install a new window in the chapel.

While the East wall did not appear to have an aperture at the time of Pugin's visit, one had certainly appeared by 1953 when Geoffrey Webb provided a characteristically sympathetic and restrained window. Unfortunately it was not seen to good advantage, due to the excess of bright light falling on it from the clear west window and more recently, because of an accretion of grime trapped between it and the external protective glass, thoughtfully but mis-guidedly provided at the time of installation.

Following competition with other artists and the eventual selection of my design, a suggestion was put forward by the church authorities to move the Webb glass to the west end, putting the new window in its place. This suggestion was firmly scotched by the Historic Churches Committee advised by the Twentieth Century Society, and I returned to the drawing board to make an amended design for the blank west window which was eventually approved by the Historic Churches Committee.

Such a small yet historic building can house few works of art or craftsmanship and the contribution of a window which has to pass the test of time and will affect the atmosphere of the chapel for centuries is not to be taken lightly. Having talked to a handful of the quarter million annual visitors and learning what their visit meant to them, there was no doubt in my mind that the window was to be designed for them. This was not the time or place for the abstract or the obscure, but what was required was a simple statement of fundamental Faith in a form instantly recognisable to every one of those entering the building.

The specified theme of the Annunciation has seen many variations since its introduction into stained glass in the 12th century, but in this case, the aim was to present the subject as a joyous event which, combined with the Centenary celebrations, could be expressed in vibrant colour and a vigorous style. If the Webb window has the restraint and delicacy of Norfolk glass of the 15th century, the new window should have the intensity and colour of much 14th century glass which would thus be in keeping with the surrounding stonework dating from the same era.

While there is appropriately a blue predominance in the window, the vision of Gabriel, firm rather than demure, is seen in a shining aura of white and gold, contrasting with the calm, if a little apprehensive, figure of Mary. Forming a canopy above her, is a "Window within a window" - a depiction of the great surviving east wall and empty window of Walsingham Priory itself - symbolic of Mary as the "Queen of Walsingham" referred to in a poignant 16th century verse lamenting the destruction of the Shrine and Priory.

The lowest sections of the window commemorate the gift of the window by The Guild of Our Lady of Ransom while above Gabriel are the moon and stars, traditional symbols of the Virgin.

The Centenary Window of the Annunciation by Alfred Fisher.

Detail of the Archangel Gabriel from the Centenary Window.

All the sections of the tracery are small and being encircled by stone work have their colour intensified. The upper three are united by a superimposed triangle representing the Trinity, cut from the now precious English gold ruby glass, repeated below in the surround of the Dove of the Holy Spirit.

The fine colour selection and glass cutting is the work of Jane Campbell, while the painting is due to the imaginative eye and hands of former partner Peter Archer of Chapel Studio at King's Langley, for whom the window was designed and who carried out the execution and installation.

The architect was Anthony Rossi.

Installation of the Centenary Window.

-

RC leader on void left by Diana death

-

1,700 at Walsingham for national pilgrimage

-

Cardinal Basil Hume, leader of the Roman Catholic Church in England and Wales, referred to the void left in many people's lives by the deaths of Diana, Princess of Wales, and Mother Theresa - without mentioning them by name - at Walsingham on Sunday.

"In these last days, there has been a sense of emptiness, loss, bewilderment, abandonment," he said in a homily to 1,700 pilgrims at Mass in the Chapel of Reconciliation.

The Cardinal, who will be 75 next year, was leading the annual Dowry of Mary national pilgrimage to the Catholics' national shrine. His concelebrants included the Bishop of East Anglia, the Rt. Rev Peter Smith; the former Bishop, the Rt Rev Alan Clark; Bishop Philip Pargeter, from Birmingham.......

In sombre mood the Cardinal started his address by saying the previous two weeks had been strange in many ways.

"Maybe the events that have struck us all so profoundly may be marking a change of mood in our nation," he said, suggesting that the Gospel could answer the questions many are asking, and give consolation to the many seeking it.

The pilgrimage, which included processing from the Chapel of Reconciliation to the Priory grounds in the centre of the village for prayers and Benediction of the Blessed Sacrament, marked the centenary of the re-establishment of national pilgrimages to Walsingham.

As Cardinal Hume is due to retire next year, Sunday's event had added significance for many. It may have been his last visit to Norfolk as the leader of English and Welsh Catholics.

Cardinal Hume at The Dowry of Mary Pilgrimage Mass, Sunday 14th September 1997.

Bishop Pargeter, Bishop Smith and Cardinal Hume, Dowry of Mary Pilgrimage,
Sunday 14th September 1997.

65

The Assumption Window in the Slipper Chapel, the work of Geoffrey Webb.

66

WEST SUSSEX COUNTY TIMES
FRIDAY NOVEMBER 21ST 1997
-

Glazed expression

-

A Horsham craftsman has done a cracking job of restoring a famous stained glass window in the "Nazareth of England."

Clifford Durrant who operates from a studio in New Street, was called in after the East Window in Walsingham's tiny Slipper Chapel began to leak.

The work of art was completed in 1953 by the famous stained glass artist Geoffrey Webb shortly before his death. But according to the magazine Church Building it was not built in the high quality craftsmanship normally associated with Mr Webb and it started to let in water.

Mr Durrant travelled to the place of pilgrimage to inspect the window and found that although the three lancets were in poor shape, the 14 small tracery lights were in good order and could easily be repaired.

The three lancets were carefully removed and brought to Horsham where photographs and rubbings of each panel were taken before they were stripped of their spent lead.

Each piece of glass was then painstakingly waterproofed with black lead cement before being returned to Walsingham, Norfolk, and reglazed. ...

"We were very honoured to be commissioned," Mr Durrant said. "We are one of only 25 accredited stained glass studios in the country."

-

BBC's "World Of Faith Week" visits Walsingham

-

Walsingham's International fame has once again brought it more valuable publicity. On this occasion, BBC's Radio 2, broadcast from the historic village as part of their World of Faith Week. In past years the Faith Week theme has provided an insight into other religions around the world, last year it concentrated on Islamic faiths. This week the fact that Walsingham is celebrating 100 years of pilgrimage earned it the opportunity to take centre stage. On Wednesday 29th October the radio presenter Debbie Thrower with the programme's production team came to Walsingham with a huge purpose built mobile recording studio. During the course of her stay in the village she interviewed a number of people and their comments were broadcast to the nation.

Scilla Landale and Jeanette King, both experienced guides of Walsingham, gave a very interesting summary of the history of the Medieval Town and some of its important landmarks. Walsingham's importance was given a boost as far back as 1226 when Henry III was King, the village was recognized as England's answer to the Holy Lands. Even today it is known as England's Nazareth.

In the 1770's the court served a wide area, and brutal punishments were meted out, including public whipping, hard labour on a treadmill, and transportation. Between 1813 and 1815 various events brought about severe hardship and increased lawlessness. This period included the end of the Napoleonic Wars, new land laws and increasing unemployment due to agricultural mechanisation.

Monsignor Anthony Stark told listeners that the Centenary marks 100 years since modern pilgrimage walks were established by Father Philip Fletcher. The 127 mile route from the City of London initially follows the A10 road then came on via Newmarket, Brandon, Swaffham and Fakenham. The most senior walker, Dr. Richard King, a retired physicist has completed the walk 34 times. The walk done by men only has been prepared like a military operation, with walkers marching in-step, in recent years this has been made difficult by modern quiet footwear.

The Crib in the Chapel of Reconciliation, Christmas 1997.

Combined Oratories Pilgrimage, Saturday 23rd May 1998.

The unveiling of the Slipper Chapel Centenary Window, (gift of the Guild of Our Lady of Ransom) by Cardinal Daly, Wednesday 20th August 1997.

The walks have also raised some £50,000 this year, and over the years, a total in excess of a million pounds, which has been given to poor country parishes.

Father Alan Williams, the Director of the Roman Catholic Shrine told of a special window that was commissioned to commemorate the centenary. When Debbie Thrower asked about Walsingham, its two shrines and overcoming the division they bring, Father Alan said "We are about the same thing and yet divided, many people go to both shrines," "there are excellent relations between the Roman Catholic and Anglican Shrines, we work together." Debbie described the village as "extraordinarily well preserved." Tom Moore, a local farmer commented "The closure of the railway had the biggest effect on Walsingham, modern day traffic with cars and coaches have caused a lot of damage to the pavements and timber framed buildings." He continued "the Parish Council is doing everything it can to try to improve the situation by keeping coaches and cars out of the street to make it better for the people who walk around and the residents who live here."

Father Keith Haydon jokingly said "Local people walk on the pavements, visitors walk in the middle of the road." It is widely recognised that tourists do create problems for local residents, but any advantage they give with employment opportunities must always be considered at the same time.

The Common Place, Anglican National Pilgrimage.

SHRINE NEWS

DECEMBER 1997 - MAY 1998

As befits the Centenary Year, there seemed to be no quiet season over the winter this year and the last few months have been a time of many "firsts". Resident groups continued to arrive well into December, albeit in smaller numbers.

During Advent and Christmas, the Shrine had a full range of services, including the very popular Annual Ecumenical Advent Carol Service. We welcomed a Weekend Retreat Group from St. John's Cathedral Norwich, who timed their visit to include this service.

Day groups started coming in January, and before the Season opened fully we had also welcomed a Residential Priests' Symposium and the East Anglian Deacon's Retreat. As part of the Music Festival, accompanying the Centenary Celebrations, the Ash Wednesday Mass was enhanced by the Choir of Ely Cathedral.

On Saturday 21st March, Walsingham went to Westminster. Westminster Cathedral, with three hundred extra seats, was full for the Centenary Mass.

The new Papal Nuncio, Archbishop Pablo Puente, was the main celebrant. Along with many clergy, including some from overseas, we were particularly pleased to welcome Bishop Alan Clark and Bishop John Rawsthorne to the Mass.

The service began with the Statue of Our Lady of Walsingham from the Slipper Chapel being carried in Procession by representatives of the Walsingham Walkers from the Guild of Our Lady Ransom, the statue was followed by representatives of many of the Major Pilgrimages to the Shrine. The Procession of Clergy stretched the length of the nave, and was a truly moving sight. The Shrine choir, augmented by other voices, led the music which included the Centenary Mass setting.

The Slipper Chapel Statue, carried by the Guild of Ransom Walkers, Westminster Cathedral, Saturday 21st March 1998.

The Sanctuary, Westminster Cathedral, Saturday 21st March 1998.

The Statue leaving the Sanctuary, Westminster Cathedral at the end of the Mass.

Fr. Shryane (King's Lynn Parish Priest), Fr. Williams, sm (Shrine Director),
Bishop Alan Clark (Bishop Emeritus of East Anglia) and His Excellency Archbishop Pablo Puente
the Apostolic Nuncio, in the Sacristy, Westminster Cathedral.

The Archbishop in his Homily recalled the history of Walsingham and the love of the Virgin Mary for English Catholics and the love of English Catholics for the Virgin Mary. In Westminster Cathedral he said we were gathered as a large family around our Mother.

Immediately after the Westminster Mass the Centenary Historical Conference took place in Walsingham. This was very well attended and the papers presented were all of a very high standard. The topics were the Foundation of the Priory, A Pilgrim's Progress to Walsingham, Medieval Pilgrimage and Healing, Remembrance of the Shrine 1538 -1897, Charlotte Boyd, the Downside Connection, the Buildings of Walsingham and Social Conditions in Victorian Walsingham. The last paper of the Conference on the Development of Modern Day Pilgrimage was presented by Canon Peter Cobb, the Master of the Anglican Guardians. They were all thought-provoking and full of information and with a great deal of humour.

The Conference papers are published as one of the Centenary Series of Publications.

Also included in the Conference Programme was a Concert by the Thames Chamber Orchestra and visits to the Anglican Shrine and King's Lynn. The latter included the King's Lynn Museum, the Catholic Church and the inside of the Red Mount Chapel.

The Feast of the Annunciation was also during the time of the Conference, when we welcomed Bishop Peter Smith. The Mass was sung by the Choir of Norwich Cathedral.

At the beginning of Holy Week we welcomed a Pilgrimage from Oscott Seminary. The Seminary has, over the years, forged many links with the Shrine, as befits a Seminary bearing the name of Our Lady. In the 1930's the Seminarians came on several Pilgrimage Retreats to Walsingham and presented the Shrine with the Processional Cross that is still in use. In July, Oscott will be lending Pilgrimage badges to the Kings Lynn Museum for its special exhibition on Pilgrimage.

Immediately after Easter, the Diocese of Plymouth came on their first Residential Pilgrimage; they were led by Bishop Christopher Budd. During their stay they included a Service of Light and a Service of Healing, as well as Masses and Processions to the Shrine.

We have been pleased to welcome many other new Residential Pilgrim Groups including members of the Association of Blind Catholics. On Low Sunday we welcomed both the Divine Mercy Pilgrims and Catholic Aids Link Pilgrimage.

The season for Major Pilgrimages usually starts at the beginning of May, with the numbers attending gradually increasing, but not this year. On 3rd May, Poland celebrates the Feast of Our Lady, Queen of Poland, so this year, as part of the Centenary Celebrations we welcomed over 2,500 Poles to the Shrine. The Pilgrimage was led by Archbishop Szczepan Wesoly, Delegate for the Primate of Poland for Poles Abroad, and many of the leaders of the Polish Community in England attended.

The Mass began with a magnificent Procession of Banners, unfortunately the bitterly cold winds meant that coats hid from view many Polish National Costumes.

In his homily the Archbishop told the congregation how, as a young man, he had taken two weeks' unpaid holiday to join the 1948 Cross Carrying Pilgrimage to Walsingham and had helped to carry the 13th Station from Leeds to Walsingham.

The Day ended with the customary Polish May Devotions and by 6 p.m. about 60 coaches and mini-buses and many cars had started on their return journeys to places such as Bolton, Bradford, Bristol, Bury and London.

The Pilgrimage from the Archdiocese of Birmingham, led by Bishop Philip Pargeter was, this year, enhanced by music from the Choir of St. Chad's Cathedral, Birmingham.

Archbishop Szczepan Wesoly, Polish Pilgrimage, Sunday 3rd May 1998.

National Costumes, Polish Pilgrimage Sunday 3rd May 1998.

The Archconfraternity of St. Stephen Pilgrimage, Monday 4th May 1998.

The Archconfraternity of St. Stephen Pilgrimage, The Abbey Grounds.

On Monday 4th May, in improved weather conditions, we welcomed another "Centenary" Pilgrimage. The National Altar Servers' Pilgrimage was led by Bishop Peter Smith. Members of the Archconfraternity of St. Stephen came and over 450 vested servers were part of the Procession for Mass. Later they went in silent Procession to the Priory Grounds and their day ended with Benediction.

We also welcomed the Pilgrimage for the Deaf, the Dominicans and the Diocese of Salford.

The Pilgrimage for the Deaf, Saturday 16th May 1998.

THE CENTENARY HISTORICAL CONFERENCE

23rd - 27th MARCH 1998

An appreciation by ANNE MILTON - Shrine Archivist

Appropriately after the delegates had travelled from many parts of the United Kingdom and from the U.S.A., the Centenary Historical Conference began on Monday 23rd March with a illustrated paper presented by Scilla Landale entitled "A Pilgrim's Progress to Walsingham." She reviewed the history of Walsingham, the reasons behind medieval Pilgrimage and outlined the Pilgrim routes to Walsingham, citing examples of the problems that faced pilgrims on their way to Walsingham. She ended with a summary of the revival of Pilgrimage to Walsingham.

The next morning Doctor Carole Rawcliffe from The Centre for East Anglian Studies, University of East Anglia, spoke on "Pilgrimage and the Sick in the Middle Ages." She considered the importance of going on Pilgrimage, the appeal of relics as a focus of a healing cult, the inadequacies of earthly medicine; the problems of diagnosis of illnesses and the strong belief in the primacy of spiritual medicine over earthly medicine throughout the medieval period. Examples were given of cures attributed to Pilgrimage and she ended by commenting "if a sick pilgrim returned home as ulcerated, feverish or lame as he or she had started out, there was, at least, some prospect of health in the life to come." That afternoon was devoted to a tour of Walsingham, led by Scilla Landale and others of the "Walsingham Guides". The subject matter of the tour was reinforced in the evening when Gerald Stocking gave a slide show and talk devoted to the "The Buildings of Walsingham."

On 25th March, the Feast of the Annunciation, Professor Christopher Harper-Bill gave a thought-provoking talk on the "Foundation and the later history of the Medieval Shrine". He examined the possible date of the foundation, Marian Devotion in the early Twelfth Century, the importance of East Anglia in medieval times (it was no rural backwater then), the history of the Augustinian Canons, the development of Pilgrimage to Walsingham and the late Medieval Priory and its end.

Timothy McDonald
Centenary Co-ordinator
introducing the
Historical Conference

Dr. Carole Rawcliffe
from the Centre of East
Anglian Studies, UEA.
"Pilgrimage and the Sick
in the Middle Ages."

Plymouth Diocese with Bishop Budd, Thursday 16th April 1998.

Northampton Diocese with Bishop McCartie, Saturday 20th June 1998.

82

Father Bill McLoughlin O.S.M. in the evening looked at "Remembrance of the Shrine 1538 - 1897." He first examined what has been restored at Walsingham since 1897 and why. He then illustrated how, despite the suppression of the Priory in 1538, remembrance of Walsingham as a holy place (and Marian devotion) had continued over the centuries. He also outlined how the lack of extant written material from the Medieval Priory, hampers research. He outlined the setting for the revival of Walsingham and the powerful personalities involved, both Roman Catholic and Anglican.

On Thursday 26th March, Ethel Hostler outlined her research on "Charlotte Boyd", the Victorian woman who purchased the Slipper Chapel, restored it, and then gave it to Downside Abbey. Miss Hostler explained that she herself was an Oblate of Malling Abbey in Kent, which was purchased in 1892 by Miss Boyd. Miss Hostler had been asked by the Prioress to discover where Miss Boyd had obtained the money for the purchase. On eventually discovering that Charlotte Boyd had been born in Macao, opium trafficking had crossed her mind, but Miss Hostler outlined how Charlotte Boyd inherited money for much philanthropic work. She outlined the effect on this work, of her being received into the Catholic Church and the problems that arose from her purchase of the Slipper Chapel.

Dom. Aidan Bellenger OSB from Downside Abbey followed with a paper on "Walsingham: Downside and the Benedictines." He outlined the Benedictine Medieval and later connections with East Anglia. He presented cameo portraits of Charlotte Boyd and many of her circle and the effect on them of late nineteenth century Benedictine monasticism. He considered the problems facing Bishop Riddell of Northampton in the context of the Diocese as a whole when Miss Boyd and friends were trying to persuade him to allow the Slipper Chapel to be used. He ended by tracing Father Bruno Scott-James's connections with Downside, the problems that faced Father Scott-James as the Priest Custodian of the Slipper Chapel and his activities after he left Walsingham.

The day ended with Howard Fears giving a paper on "Social Conditions in Victorian Walsingham." He outlined the conditions of life in Victorian Walsingham and changes that took place. He gave examples of the quality of life, the problems of overcrowding, the scarcity of steady work, the decline of craft workers and the attempts at unionisation. He outlined the growth of the temperance movement and the influence of the religious denominations in Victorian Walsingham. The coming of the railway to Walsingham and its consequences concluded his talk.

The Conference ended with Canon Peter Cobb, Master of the College of Guardians of the Anglican Shrine surveying "The Development of Modern Day Pilgrimage." Canon Cobb looked at the reasons behind the restoration of the Shrine to Our Lady of Walsingham in King's Lynn, and the later transfer of the Shrine to the Slipper Chapel. He explained the background behind the revival of Pilgrimage to Walsingham among the Anglicans and the growth and the problems of the development of the Anglican devotion. He then surveyed the growth of both Shrines and ecumenical developments that had taken place in Walsingham.

The Shrine has published the Conference papers

"Walsingham - Pilgrimage and History"

Available from:

Roman Catholic National Shrine
The Pilgrim Bureau
Friday Market
Walsingham
NR22 6EG

The Altar of Repose in the Slipper Chapel, Maundy Thursday 1998.

The Slipper Chapel, Good Friday 1998.

Student Cross, Northern Leg crossing the Stiffkey in flood, Good Friday 1998.

Student Cross in Friday Market on Good Friday 1998.

DEREHAM AND FAKENHAM TIMES
THURSDAY APRIL 9th 1998

Birthday Walkers arriving

Walkers will be converging on Walsingham tomorrow after long pilgrimages from many English towns.

And this year's Student Cross pilgrimage is a special one, marking the 50th anniversary of the first walk from the University of London in 1948.

To commemorate the occasion, each of nine groups is carrying a celebration cross, engraved with a commemorative logo, which will be sited permanently in the grounds of the Roman Catholic Shrine of Our Lady.

On the walkers' arrival on Good Friday, they will join together with some of the original 1948 pilgrims to celebrate Easter. One of the walkers from the early days, Dr. John Bryden has written a history of the pilgrimage, "Behold the Wood."

"Student Cross has brought a real joy to many, many people over the 50 years and enabled them to realise they can enjoy their faith and celebrate it." said Chris Awre, National Organiser for 1998. "The pilgrimage is one of the most alive ways I know of celebrating Easter. It has inspired people for 50 years now and I am sure it will continue to do so for the next 50."

Legs of the pilgrimage started in Colchester, Epping, Oxford, Desborough, Leicester and Keyworth. A shorter, three-day leg started in Ely, there is a local one-day leg from North Elmham and even a King's Lynn based peg-leg for family groups.

Along the way, pilgrims have been sleeping in village halls, fed and encouraged by local parishioners.

The walks are interspersed with times of silence, prayer, music and singing. Culmination of the event is a Vigil service on Saturday night, followed by an all-night party, a Sunday morning communion and a procession around Walsingham.

EASTERN DAILY PRESS
FRIDAY APRIL 10th 1998

-

Pilgrims wend their way to Walsingham Shrine

-

Hundreds of foot-weary people descend on the village of Walsingham today at the end of an Easter pilgrimage.

Groups of walkers carrying crosses set out from around Britain as early as last Saturday, to meet in the Norfolk pilgrim centre this afternoon.

This year is the 50th Student Cross pilgrimage and about 300 people, including some from as far afield as Mexico, are taking part.

They have slept in church halls, been fed by local parishioners, and have had times of prayer, silence and singing.

There is a vigil service tomorrow, followed by an all-night party, a Sunday communion and a procession around Walsingham.

Each of the nine groups is carrying a celebration cross, engraved with a logo, which will be sited permanently in the grounds of the Roman Catholic Shrine of Our Lady.

The 28 people on the Northern leg, which set out from Nottingham, will have walked 120 miles by the time they reach Walsingham today.

Andrea Watts, on her 30th Student Cross pilgrimage said: "It is a complete break from normal life.

The atmosphere is very good and we are looking forward to the Easter Weekend." Emma Simcock, a full time volunteer worker from Manchester, is on her first pilgrimage.

"I came along not knowing anyone, but I have been really warmly welcomed."

The Student Cross 50th Anniversary Cross.

The Centenary Festival of Flowers, 22nd - 25th May 1998.
St. Mary's Anglican Parish Church.

-

Festival Blooming

-

The flower festival season bursts into colourful life next weekend, with many of them starting on Friday. One of the biggest is at Walsingham, where six different chapels and churches are taking part in an event which marks a centenary of pilgrimage to the National Shrine. Roman Catholic, Anglican and Methodist churches are taking part.

The festival has been designed by Margaret Peel, of Fakenham, and will be opened by the Duchess of Norfolk, during the noon Mass on Friday. Mass will be celebrated by the retired Bishop of East Anglia, the Rt Rev Alan Clark.

During the afternoon the Duchess will visit the various churches taking part in the festival, and at 7.30 the choir of Farm Street Church, conducted by Martin Parry, will give a concert. Actress Liza Goddard will give readings, and David Graham will play the organ......

The Sanctuary in The Slipper Chapel.

DEREHAM AND FAKENHAM TIMES
THURSDAY MAY 21st 1998

Imported blooms set to save the big day

-

By JOHN BULTITUDE

-

The team behind a floral celebration of Norfolk's spiritual heart have gone Dutch after a quirk of nature jeopardised their best blooms.

A 63-strong team is preparing displays for the Festival of Flowers which opens tomorrow in Walsingham to celebrate 100 years of pilgrimage to the village.

But poor UK growing conditions meant they had to order 10,000 blooms from Holland to decorate six churches and chapels in the village. Margaret Peel, Festival Designer, explained: "We did try to buy them in this country, but there was so much low light last month that the flowers did not grow sufficiently and are just not ready."

The festival, which has the theme of elegance and simplicity, links with the current centenary celebrations at the shrine.

Mrs Peel has spent 12 months working on the display, which is believed to be the biggest of its type in Norfolk.

She said: "I have done many flower festivals over the years and raised a lot of money in the process of doing so but this is the largest I have ever undertaken." She said the Duchess of Norfolk would be officially opening this Centenary Festival of Flowers.

The public can visit the six chapels and churches decorated with flowers from 10 am to 5 pm over the Bank Holiday weekend.

They are the Chapel of Reconciliation and Slipper Chapel at the Roman Catholic Shrine; the Anglican Shrine and Holy House; St Mary's Anglican Parish Church; Walsingham Methodist Church and the Roman Catholic Church of the Annunciation.

Fr. Alfred Hope Patten's original grave memorial, St. Mary's Anglican Parish Church.

The Tabernacle arrangement, Chapel of Reconciliation.

The Original 1897 Pilgrimage Poster arrangement.

94

FAKENHAM AND DISTRICT SUN
JUNE 1998

-

Walsingham Flower Festival

-

Walsingham was awash with flowers for the May Bank Holiday weekend as the Roman Catholic National Shrine held a "Festival of Flowers" during its "Pilgrimage Centenary Year." The Festival was designed by Margaret Peel of Fakenham. Margaret was born in Walsingham and is well-known in Norfolk flower arranging circles.

Six churches were decorated for the Festival. The Slipper Chapel and the Chapel of Reconciliation at the Roman Catholic Shrine, the Anglican Parish Church of St Mary's, the Methodist Chapel, the R. C. Parish Church of the Annunciation and the Anglican Shrine.

Her Grace the Duchess of Norfolk read the lesson at the Opening Mass in the Chapel of Reconciliation which was celebrated by the retired Bishop of East Anglia the Rt. Rev. Alan Clark, and sung by the world famous choir of Farm Street Church, London. The Farm Street Singers gave a concert in St. Mary's Parish Church on Friday evening as part of the Centenary Concert Series.

During the afternoon, the Duchess of Norfolk visited the six churches and talked to the various flower arrangers, some of whom were individuals and some had come from Holt, Fakenham, Costessey and Dereham Flower Clubs, as well as students from Easton College.

The visit started at St. Mary's where Fr. Keith Haydon was her guide - she then went to the Methodist Chapel where she met Rev. John and Cathy Bushell from Canada who are on an exchange with Rev. Jonathon Haigh, the Methodist Minister. After a visit to the R. C. Parish Church, the Duchess was met at the Anglican Shrine by the Administrator, Fr. Martin Warner, who, after a tour of the Holy House and Shrine Church, hosted a tea party in the College.

-

Duchess visits Flower Festival

-

The Duchess of Norfolk was in Walsingham at the weekend to officially open the village's flower festival. It was a special occasion as it was apart of the centenary celebrations of the re-dedication of the Catholic shrine. Also in the village was the former Catholic Bishop of East Anglia, the Rt. Rev Alan Clark, who celebrated Mass to mark the start of the festival.

There were over 100 displays, designed by 63 different arrangers adding colour to the six churches in the village, said Centenary Co-ordinator Timothy McDonald. He added; "It is difficult to estimate how many people came along, as the weekend also marked the Anglican [National] Pilgrimage, but everybody seemed impressed with what they saw." The event had taken 18 months and a lot of hard work to organise, and he was pleased with how successful the weekend had been. Mr McDonald thanked Walsingham woman Mrs Margaret Peel who chose the designs.

"All the six churches had sanctuaries and high altars dressed in white flowers to show unity between the churches," he added. "There was no particular theme for the festival, but the displays were very imaginative," he said. "Although this was part of the Roman Catholic celebration, every denomination in Walsingham benefited from this colourful weekend ," he said.

The Duchess of Norfolk reading the Lesson during the Opening Mass of The Festival of Flowers, 22nd May 1998.

The Church of the Annunciation, Friday Market.

The Methodist Chapel, the "R" for Rome arrangement.

97

Bishop Alan Clark,
Bishop Emeritus of East Anglia.

The Replica Statue arrangement,
The Church of the Annunciation.

**HOMILY PREACHED BY
THE RT. REV. ALAN CLARK DD,
BISHOP EMERITUS OF EAST ANGLIA
Friday May 22nd 1998**

*At the Chapel of Reconciliation, Walsingham on the occasion of the Opening
of the Centenary Festival of Flowers (the day of the Irish Referendum for
Peace).*

My Beloved friends. By way of anticipating what will be said much better
later in this Mass, I do wish to signify the welcome that we are happy to offer
all of you, by coming today to celebrate this first day of the Flower Festival,
in order that we may indeed understand the wonder, the tenderness and the
joy of Mary. In particular, one would want to welcome Her Grace the
Duchess of Norfolk, who has come with her Sister-in-law [Lady Marigold
Jamieson] to be here today. And we also would like to send His Grace our
warmest wishes and the fact that we miss him and hope that he will soon
recover the best of health. And the welcome goes to all of us, here today,
who have come with a great sense of tranquillity and sweetness in our hearts
to this celebration of the flowers of the field and flowers that have been
engendered by the skill of men and women. All these may display to us the
greatness and the beauty of God.

In the pilgrim Centenary Brochure you will find on this day many wonderful
things said about the deep binding of the flowers of the field to Mary. In the
days when the flowers that are now bought by us from our gardens, were
non-existent. The flowers of the field were there and so Mary's name was
joined to them and we think with wonder of the lily.

Our God himself was caught by its beauty "the lilies of the field they neither
toil nor do they spin but not even Solomon," the greatest figure in the Jewish
history of the Kings of Israel, "not even Solomon was arrayed like one of
these." Our Lord himself was caught up in rapturous appreciation of the
greatness of God in creating a flower, the lily, which through the hard and
generous labour of the flower arrangers are scattered around this church,
around the village, everywhere in all the churches of Walsingham, where we
may look at them and say "My God, I thank you for the beauty of your
creation, the beauty which somehow supports us in times of anguish, times
when the burden is very heavy."

And we think most of all today of the flower of peace, in making a gift of Our Lady to our countries on this day in particular. The flower of peace. God in his great goodness and in the tremendous creativity of his fields created a whole mass of thousands and thousands of beautiful blooms and blossoms to show us his own beauty - a beauty which is reflected in Mary, his daughter.

And we have come here - loving her - seeking from her the gifts that we need today in this ravelled world. In these particular days we want a great gift through the intercession of Mary of Walsingham.

For all of us are of one mind here. You do not have to conjure up thoughts, you just say "Mary, Mother of God, Mother of Men, Mother of all that is created, come to us, be among us, in order that we may see with your eyes the greatness of the God whose world this is, who is in this world and he longs to put it into the way of eternal salvation."

But we have our mission there, all of us today, a mission to carry on that mission begun by the Apostles who gathered in the Upper Room whose names we heard and that we should continue in the way we live, in the sign we give, and in the love we show. And when we turn to Mary, our hearts really are too full, too full of the wonder of it all.

And so, my beloved friends it is such a joy to look round upon you today - to know the labour of the flower arrangers, that they have made this such a beautiful sight for our eyes.

For we will see more today as we look at the other churches, so that one great gathering of flowers are here in Walsingham, such as never has been seen before. It is then, an historic day, bringing us all together to honour Mary - Queen, Mary in her month of May. She is indeed the sweetest and most tender of women, and she understands the hearts of men and women and children. Pray to her that she may encourage them to stand firm in their faith, and God knows we need an increase of faith, and also an increase of love and in particular for all those throughout the world who are tending to the starving and the dying. Please, Mary, help them, encourage them, give them the heart such as you have, so that they may bring these poor suffering nations of the world to a time of peace and tranquillity.

How much more can be said - for one would need a poet to do it - one would need a Gerard Manley-Hopkins to say it - but we say it in our own humble way. Let it spill out of our lips, let it come from our tongue with the assuredness that God himself is in our presence today just as we are in His presence. And Mary herself walks with us - particularly as we salute as brethren all these gatherings of flowers, all these gatherings of prayer - that will be the continuance of this day.

I did not mention at the beginning our appreciation of the coming of the Choir of Farm Street. What a joy you have given us - always sing as you have sung today.

And may there be a particular blessing on the Marist Fathers, who with the help of the Sisters, and of their many helpers in the village and elsewhere, enable this Shrine to be a beacon of hope and of love and of strength to the Nation - not just to us. And so may these days of celebration - these Festival days be a memory never forgotten in the history of Walsingham.

The Icon of The Mother of God of Walsingham arrangement

The Sacred Heart arrangement,
The Church of the Annunciation.

Rev. Alan Williams, sm

**WORDS SPOKEN BY
REV. ALAN WILLIAMS SM,
DIRECTOR OF THE NATIONAL SHRINE OF OUR LADY,
WALSINGHAM
Friday May 22nd 1998**

At the Chapel of Reconciliation at the end of the Solemn Mass opening the Centenary Festival of Flowers

Since last August, we have been celebrating our Centenary here at the National Shrine at Walsingham and I think today is a particular joy to me, as it brings together all the churches of Walsingham. The Anglican, Methodist and Roman Catholic communities have had a very long tradition of working together in Walsingham, and I think the Flower Festival today and over this coming weekend will do even more for practical ecumenism on the ground. It is so important for all our visitors, for all our Pilgrims.

Bishop Alan has mentioned one or two names - one or two welcomes. But if I can say thank you to the Duchess of Norfolk for being with us today to open the Flower Festival - I am aware that His Grace is not with us. The Duke is one of our Patrons - but we are entirely with him in our thoughts and our prayers. Bishop Alan Clark is, of course, a great friend of the Shrine. When the Centenary was being planned, Bishop Alan was very much at the helm - so I am delighted that His Lordship is with us today. And we do have with us ecumenical guests from the various churches. Fr. Keith Haydon, who is the Parish Priest of St. Mary's Anglican Parish Church; we also welcome Fr. Colin who is representing the Anglican Shrine - and also Rev. Jim Bushell, a Canadian Methodist Minister working in North Norfolk.

One or two other names I would like to mention. We have the St. Mary's, Monmouth Pilgrimage today with us, who are here with Fr. David Smith; the Chorley Deanery Pilgrimage and also the Skegness Pilgrimage who are here with Fr. Finneran. For those of you who like one or two names from the Altar, we have with us Fr. Charles, a Passionist Priest who is chaplain to the North London Walsingham Association. We also have with us Fr. Austin Horsley sm, and if I may say so, if Bishop Alan is described as Bishop Emeritus now, then let me tell you Austin is Provincial Emeritus - he is a much calmer man now that he has retired. And also from the Shrine we have Fr. Jarvis and Fr. Rear.

I have already been overawed by what little I have seen - but I notice that in the programme for today and for the weekend, Margaret Peel, Festival Designer says she characterises this Flower Festival by two words - "Elegance and Simplicity" (laughter) …. Indeed - but I suspect, Margaret, that many other words will be used over the weekend. I think it is beyond words - it is wonderful - so Margaret and all your helpers - thank you very much indeed - I think it is delightful - wonderful. And of course, our music - we have had with us the Farm Street Choir - they have been absolutely marvellous......

And to anyone else I have not mentioned, or have forgotten, have an even more wonderful Flower Festival than the rest of us - God bless you.

Seed Collage of King Henry VIII, Barsham Manor, and the Slipper Chapel.

The Font arrangements at St. Mary's.

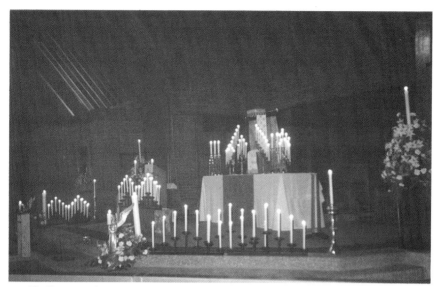

The Sanctuary during the Forty Hours Devotion, June 1998.

Corpus Christi Procession, Sr. Monica Tierney, sm (left) and Sr. Rose Revilles, sm

June heralded even more Pilgrimages but unfortunately not summer weather. We welcomed the Catholic Women's League Pilgrimage led by Bishop Walmsley on Saturday 6th June. In this year of the Holy Spirit he reminded us in his homily that *"the same Holy Spirit which revealed Yahweh to Moses, which ignited the flames of Sinai, which came down as a dove on Jesus in the Jordan, which transformed the Apostles at Pentecost and caused Mary to conceive God, is the very same Spirit. ...who now empowers us to carry Christ into the world"*. He called on the members to pledge themselves to work for the reorganisation and renewal of the Catholic Women's League *"It will be renewed only if you generously permit the Holy Spirit to work in you and through you."* The next day Hallam Diocese came on Pilgrimage, followed on Monday 8th June by seminarians from Allen Hall Seminary, who came to Walsingham as part of our Centenary Celebrations.

Corpus Christi this year was marked with a 40 Hours Exposition of the Blessed Sacrament. During a candlelit Holy Hour of music and prayer, which incorporated a memorable performance of Mendelssohn's Lauda Sion, members of the congregation placed votive candles on the altar steps. Exposition continued through the night, and included devotions at midnight, 4.00 a.m. and 8.00 a.m. On the Feast of Corpus Christi we welcomed Bishop Leo McCartie of Northampton as Principal Celebrant for Solemn Mass sung by the Boy's Choir of Ely Cathedral. Bad weather meant the Blessed Sacrament Procession had to be inside. The 40 hours ended with a moving Benediction. We would like to thank all who joined us for this special time, our resident pilgrims, all who maintained the watch and those who enhanced the time with their music.

On Saturday 13th June we were joined by pilgrims from Brentwood Diocese and a Vocations Pilgrimage. This day was tinged by sadness with the news of the sudden death of Sister Monica S.M., one of the Marist sisters who worked at the Shrine. She was remembered in the prayers of all the pilgrims that day, and the next when the Diocese of East Anglia, joined by some members of the Knights of Malta came on Pilgrimage.

After having processed along the Holy Mile, there was a time for picnic lunch that was enjoyed in bright sunshine. Unfortunately this did not last and during Mass the skies opened. Most had come prepared for the 'English summer', and after putting on wet weather gear, stood their ground.

However, by the next day the weather improved and we welcomed schools for the Primary Schools' Pilgrimage, including a group from Kirkby on Merseyside. After Mass and various activities they joined in a procession. Bishop McCartie returned to the Shrine to lead the Northampton Pilgrimage on Saturday 20th June. Having had a hip replacement operation in the Spring, all his pilgrims were pleased to see him walking the Holy Mile. Members of the Guild of St. Agatha, the Catholic Association of Bell Ringers, who were spending a weekend in the area also joined the Northampton Mass. On Sunday 21st June, the Archdiocese of Birmingham Catholic Handicapped Fellowship led by Bishop Philip Pargeter came to celebrate their 40th Anniversary and join our Centenary Celebrations. The next week, steel drums were the order of the day when the Caribbean Pilgrimage made its annual visit.

At the beginning of July, we welcomed many friends for the Marist Pilgrimage, led again by Father Joachim Fernandez, Superior General of the Marist Fathers. A group from Germany led by Father Dennis Green S.M. joined the Pilgrimage. Thankfully those who joined the Pilgrimage for the Sick enjoyed pleasant weather. This Pilgrimage is always a touching sight with the Sacrament of the Sick during Mass, and Bishop Peter Smith moving around the grounds blessing all with the Blessed Sacrament during the Benediction.

After last year's problems, the weather was better for the 53rd Annual U.C.M. Pilgrimage. Many gathered for a torchlight service at the Shrine on the Monday evening. The Pilgrimage was led by Bishop Terence Brain of Salford in his role as Spiritual Adviser to the U.C.M. Each year, in alphabetical rotation, one Diocese is the 'Lead Diocese' for the U.C.M. Pilgrimage. It so happened that during Walsingham's Centenary Celebrations, this year it was the turn of East Anglia. So along with all members of the U.C.M. from East Anglia who could possibly attend, we again welcomed Bishop Peter Smith to the Shrine. During the Mass, the U.C.M. presented two chalices, one of which was a specially commissioned Centenary Chalice and complements the Centenary Chalice presented last August by members of the Wolverhampton Branch of the Walsingham Association.

The Caribbean Pilgrimage, Steel Band, Sunday 28th June 1998.

The UCM Chalice and the Centenary Chalice being presented Tuesday 7th July 1998.

Pilgrimage of Reconciliation and Consecration, Saturday 11th July 1998.

The Tamil Pilgrimage Procession, Sunday 19th July 1998.

The Fifth Pilgrimage of Reparation and Consecration was led by Bishop Vincent Nichols. In the Priory Grounds he reconsecrated England and Wales to the Immaculate Heart of Mary almost 50 years to the day after Cardinal Griffin had first consecrated England and Wales at the end of the 1948 Cross Carrying Pilgrimage. The 50th Anniversary of the cross carrying pilgrimage was celebrated on 17th July.

The following weekend, we were joined by representatives of the Order of Carmelites and the Order of Discalced Carmelites for a Joint Pilgrimage to celebrate our Centenary. The next day ... over 4,000 members of the Tamil Community came to share a day at the Shrine. The day began with a procession then Mass was celebrated mainly in Tamil. After a shared meal and a time of fellowship their day ended with Benediction....

We were pleased, once again, to welcome supporters of the St. Patrick's Missionary Society for one of their annual Mission days. After Mass, they had a talk about the work of the Kiltegan Fathers, particularly in the Caribbean and their day ended with Benediction. On Saturday 1st August both Shrines in Walsingham welcomed representatives from the Lambeth Bishop's Conference. Over 50 Bishops and other participants from the Conference visited the Anglican Shrine and then came to the R. C. Shrine and joined in Prayers for Unity, appropriately in the Chapel of Reconciliation, before making a visit to the Slipper Chapel for private prayer.

The 12th New Dawn Conference at the beginning of August was a step of faith for the organisers, who, working on the basis of Isaiah 55:1 - *"Oh, come to the water all you who are thirsty; though you have no money, come"* - this year charged no set conference fee. They asked all to pay what they were able, in order not to deter those who were not able to pay the normal conference fee. Numbers appeared to have increased and, after the first day, summer also seemed to arrive in Walsingham. The growing freedom of religious expression in Eastern European countries was reflected in the attendance of delegations from both the Czech and Slovak Republics, and the first attendees from Russia. On the Monday evening, there was the traditional welcome, and a talk by Dave Matthews, the first non-Catholic speaker at the Conference. There were evening services of healing and reconciliation and daily workshops and talks. The conference participants processed along the old railway track into Walsingham for Mass in the Priory Grounds on Wednesday, and the next day, the traditional Mass in the Shrine grounds was celebrated. The preacher at this Mass was the Franciscan Father, Stan Fortuna. This year, the prayer continued after the end of the normal conference sessions, with well-attended Exposition of the Blessed Sacrament in the Chapel of Reconciliation throughout each night. The family camp has increased in popularity and there is a separate youth ministry for those aged 12-25 with a special programme for younger children during most of the day.

The New Dawn week ended with the Walsingham Centenary Youth Festival at the Shrine. This was a time of shared prayer, Christian rock bands playing, a special Mass and the day ended with a barbecue.

The next week we welcomed 400 youngsters for the four day Ecumenical Youth Pilgrimage. On Friday 14th August, there was a Centenary Party for the Assumption at the Shrine, with a Barbecue, a Jazz Band, Barbershop Singers and a local line dancing team. On Saturday 15th August, the Annual Assumptiontide Lecture on "Marian Devotion in the Scandinavian Churches" was given by Dean Leif Norrgard. That evening, Christians of all denominations joined together for the Asssumption Ecumenical Torchlight Procession of Witness. During the following week, Bishop Ambrose Griffiths was the Main Celebrant and Preacher at Mass on 19th August, the 101st Anniversary of the re-founding of the Shrine.

On Saturday 5th September, we welcomed the Diocese of Leeds, and the next day we were joined by Liverpool Archdiocese and the Norwich Anglican Diocesan Families Pilgrimage accompanied by two donkeys. On 7th September, the Centenary Festival Week began. Throughout the week there was a daily Solemn Mass and Vespers, and a Concert followed by Sung Compline. Tuesday 8th was the Feast of the Birthday of the Blessed Virgin Mary, and the Right Reverend Charles Fitzgerald-Lombard of Downside, a Centenary Patron was Chief Celebrant at the Pilgrim Mass.

The Centenary ended with two major Pilgrimages. On the 11th, we welcomed members of the Servite Order on a residential weekend pilgrimage and on Sunday 13th September it was The Dowry of Mary Pilgrimage, which would close the Centenary Celebrations led by Cardinal Hume. The day started overcast and windy, with the worst weather forecast in the country for north Norfolk. It was very cold, and we all remembered with longing the heat of August 1997 and the beginning of the Centenary Celebrations, 13 months previously.

The Ecumenical Youth Pilgrimage, 9th-13th August 1998.

The Ecumenical Procession for the Assumption, Saturday 15th August 1998.

Rt Rev Thomas McMahon, Bishop of Brentwood.

HOMILY PREACHED BY
THE RT. REV. THOMAS McMAHON
BISHOP OF BRENTWOOD
SATURDAY 13th JUNE 1998.

This year I cannot help but take the theme of 'pilgrimage' - after all, it is the Centenary year of the first Catholic pilgrimage since the Reformation and people have been coming here as pilgrims for close on one thousand years.

Each of us is unique, yet the story of any one of us is, in some measure, the story of us all. That is certainly true of the Christian family and 'journeying' or 'pilgrimage' is a very biblical word. I think of Abraham called by God to leave his home and country and to go out he knew not where. I imagine Abraham just made the same excuses that we all make. Abraham telling God that he was doing very useful work at Ur and he couldn't really be spared. Abraham telling God that he was not quite sure that he was hearing God's call correctly and clearly. Abraham wondering whether he had got the whole thing utterly wrong. Abraham at length, being honest with God and saying how much he feared to go into the unknown and leave behind security, people, things that were precious to him and familiar and made him feel comfortable. Then, finally Abraham leaving Ur, trusting God, and allowing himself to be moved on to whatever God had in mind for him. It was a new beginning by which he would glorify God and be the father of all believers.

I think of the Israelites journeying through the desert to the promised land for 40 years, complaining at times that they would rather go back to where they came from. On the journey, God strove to teach His people repentance, faith and trust.

How often we have felt like them, weary from the burden and impatient to see the journey's end; tempted to doubt God's providence and to question His care, we may become anxious and question whether it is all worth it, but once again He seeks to teach us these same three things.

In the New Testament we read that all faithful Jewish men were expected to attend at least one of the three pilgrimage feasts during the course of the year (Passover, Pentecost, Tabernacles) and Jesus like every obedient son of Moses, did just this.

Christians, like those of other Faiths, have always gone on pilgrimage. I think it has to do with two things:-

(1) *A search for roots.* A few months ago we had a classic example, post-war orphans returning to Britain from Western Australia after fifty years to discover members of their families whom they never knew existed. And these people, so the reports tell us, referred to their journey as 'pilgrimage'. The search for roots meets a deep human hunger. By discovering where we come from, we have a chance to discover who we are.

(2) A further reason why a certain place is regarded as holy and people come on pilgrimage is because it is there that people seek *to encounter God and His Holy Mother.*

It has certainly been so in the case of Walsingham in the thousand years of its existence and a hundred years of Catholic pilgrimage it was in 1061 that a lady called Richeldis, of the Manor nearby, had a vision of Our Lady whilst at prayer, and was inspired to build a shrine, a simple replica of the Holy House of Nazareth where Jesus spent his childhood. It is said (like Lourdes) that a spring of water appeared to indicate the site on which the house was to be built and this became one of the four great Shrines of Europe, ranking with Rome, Jerusalem and Compostella. In the 12th century, Augustinian Canons came to look after the Shrine and built a Priory. People left their shoes at the Slipper Chapel and walked bare-footed into the Holy Land of Walsingham. Sadly, it was destroyed by the very King who used to come here on pilgrimage.

Devotion lived on, albeit secretly and it was at the end of the last century that Charlotte Boyd bought the Slipper Chapel and restored it at her own cost and gave it back to the Church. In 1921 Father Hope Patten became Vicar of Walsingham and set up a statue modelled on the Priory seal. Pilgrims came in numbers, both Anglican and Roman Catholic and the Holy House was rebuilt. In 1934, the Roman Catholic Bishops declared the Slipper Chapel to be, once again, the National Shrine of Our Lady.

Pilgrimage reminds us, as we read in 1 Peter, that we are only 'visitors' and 'pilgrims' here below. As we travel the road, in our mind's eye we see someone coming towards us - it is Christ, beckoning us to be ever closer to Him who is the Way, the Life and the Truth. Above all, remember all along the journey that our destination and our companion are one.

The floodlit Slipper Chapel.

The 50th Anniversary Cross Carrying Pilgrimage, The Altar, Chapel of Reconciliation, Friday 17th July 1998.

Fr. Alan Williams welcoming Bishop Ambrose Griffiths and the Cross Carrying Pilgrims, Friday 17th July 1998.

118

CATHOLIC HERALD
FRIDAY JULY 31st 1998

Commemorating Walsingham 1948

-

By DERMOT DORAN (Cross IV 1948)

-

The Climax to last week's 50th anniversary commemoration of the 1948 Cross Carrying Pilgrimage to Walsingham......was the Pontifical Concelebrated Mass alongside the 600-year-old Slipper Chapel [containing the statue] of Our Lady of Walsingham.

Bishop Ambrose Griffiths, who as a young lad had been one of the cross-carrying pilgrims, set the scene of the time: "When in 1948 some 400 people walked 200 or more miles carrying heavy crosses in pilgrimage to this holy place we hoped to see the end of war and the gift of real peace...But even as we walked, a major wartime ally was changing into a most dangerous enemy, the Cold War had begun and conflicts were already raging in Palestine and elsewhere."

In 1948, 14 solid-oak crosses, one for each Station of the Cross, were carried over a two-week period, from 14 points in England and Wales to Walsingham. On the final day, July 16, 1948, the feast of Our Lady of Mount Carmel, 15,000 other pilgrims from all over the country (and students from Boulogne) joined them for the unforgettable ceremonies, led by Cardinal Griffin, to conclude PPP 1948, the Pilgrimage of Prayer and Penance for Peace.

The Berlin Airlift had just started - to relieve Soviet-besieged Berlin, 60 Super-fortress bombers were flying from the United States to RAF stations in Britain, including that at Marham, about 20 miles from Walsingham. The *Herald* front page of July 9 [1948] gave equal prominence to PPP 1948 and an interview with Cardinal Mindszenty, Primate of Hungary, on communist persecution of the Church in his country (which was to develop into his own persecution).

In 1998 some 30 of those cross-carrying pilgrims of 1948 came again to Walsingham - with wives, relatives and representatives of those who have died, some 200 pilgrims in all. On this occasion all but one used modern transport. The exception was a 72 year old veteran of 1948 (and many later pilgrimages) who came again on foot - all the way from, appropriately, Canterbury.

Each of the 30 former foot-pilgrims had a part to play in the anniversary programme. The 14 crosses standing in the grounds of the Slipper Chapel are, of course, the crosses we carried in 1948. So when all the 1998 pilgrims made the Stations of the Cross on the evening of our arrival, a 1948 cross carrier delivered the appropriate scriptural reading at each station - and also at the later 15th station signifying the Resurrection. Then, at the Pontifical Concelebrated Mass, all but one of the celebrants were 1948 cross carriers - the additional celebrant being Fr. Alan Williams, the present Director of the National Shrine of Our Lady [at] Walsingham. Other cross carriers of 50 years ago participated in other functions and I had the privilege of delivering the first reading.

Here special mention must be made of the person who was chosen for the second reading, a lady, Eileen Lovas. In 1948 several ladies were among the local parishioners who helped carry crosses for short distances into and out of parish churches visited on the various routes, but Eileen did more: she was one of the three young schoolgirls, the "truant trio" who helped carry Cross I (Westminster) for most of three days through Essex - though it must be recorded that their collective truancy was condoned.

Perhaps the most nostalgic event was a symbolic re-enactment of 1948. Another, lighter, cross was carried in procession from the Slipper Chapel along the "Holy Mile" (which is more than a mile) to the Walsingham Priory grounds for the final Benediction. It was carried horizontally, as in 1948, with two at the front supporting the cross beam on their shoulders and one behind supporting the foot.

I took my turn at the front with Bishop Ambrose (we were paired off by height, not holiness) and, also symbolically, three brand-new young men carried the cross into the Priory grounds. The Benediction, mostly in 1948-style Latin, was given by Mgr John Furnival, son of 1948 cross carrier Joe Furnival who also participated.

Bishop Ambrose Griffiths and other 1948 veterans.

The Benediction, Abbey Grounds, Friday 17th July 1998.

The 1948 Veterans, Abbey Grounds, Friday 17th July 1998.

The 1948 Veterans, Abbey Grounds, Friday 17th July 1998.

122

Walsingham, is, of course, a centre of pilgrimage also for the Church of England - and the Anglican shrine there should not be missed on a visit - so was it just ecumenical coincidence that at 4 o'clock, as the Monstrance was elevated to outline the four points of the cross, we could just hear four perfectly timed chimes from the clock tower of Walsingham's parish church of St. Mary's?

Other "coincidences" were carefully planned: Mgr. Furnival was secretary to the late Archbishop Derek Worlock, who, as Fr Derek Worlock, participated in PPP 1948 as secretary to Cardinal Griffin.

Mgr. Furnival had earlier spoken on the inspiration behind PPP 1948, "a miracle of organisation and a great act of courage," by Charles Osborne as a "magnificent response to the call of Pope Pius XII for an act of reparation and repentance after World War II".

We were reminded later how Charles Osborne's participation in the 1946 pilgrimage - carrying a cross to Vézelay in France - had prompted him to organise and lead a similar pilgrimage carrying a cross from Bishop's Stortford to Walsingham in 1947 as a rehearsal for PPP 1948, and how PPP 1948 had been actively supported nationwide by the Union of Catholic Mothers. Fr. Columba Ryan conveyed a special message of greeting from Charles' 99-year-old widow Ursula, and we were joined by their son Major Miles Osborne and his wife. We were also reminded of the annual Student Cross pilgrimages which also started in 1948, and the Guild of Ransom pilgrimages. PPP 1948 men figured in them all.

The inspired and indefatigable 1998 organiser was 1948 pilgrim John Lyons who, 50 years ago, helped carry Cross XI from Birkenhead - and his "backer" was Mgr. Furnival. It was John who organised the production of the elaborately illuminated, hand-crafted Walsingham Book as a record of PPP 1948 and then led the 1992 walk to carry it from Birkenhead to Walsingham. (I took part at each end of this mini-pilgrimage - but not the hard bit in the middle.)

In 1948 the weather ranged from very wet to very hot - presumably that was part of the penance. But last week Our Lady of the Weather took care of us: it rained only when we were indoors, it was cool when we carried the "lightweight" cross, and it was brilliantly sunny for Benediction in the Priory grounds. There was prayer certainly, but no real penance this time (except for those who walked), thanks to the wonderful work of the tireless staff at the Walsingham Shrine and the excellent accommodation and meals in the pilgrim centre.

No words can adequately describe how we instantly resumed the Christianity and comradeship of 1948 - and how we appreciated the short presentations from personal diaries and recollections. We all have - or at least have seen - many of the press photographs of the time, but were enthralled to see a video made from a previously "lost" ciné film, in black and white of course, recently discovered by Mgr. Pat Corrigan of Banbury.

The 1998 Commemoration of PPP fitted neatly into the current year of events for the centenary of the restoration of the Shrine of Our Lady of Walsingham, the history of which goes back to 1061, five years before William the Conqueror and not long after a previous millennium. There was certainly talk of PPP 2000.

The XVth Station decorated during the Festival of Flowers.

The 1998 Cross Carriers, 'the brand new young men'
the 50th Anniversary Cross Carrying Pilgrimage.

Bishop Ambrose Griffiths, Bishop of Hexham and Newcastle..

HOMILY PREACHED BY
THE RT. REV. AMBROSE GRIFFITHS, OSB, MA, BSc.
BISHOP OF HEXHAM AND NEWCASTLE.
Friday July 17th 1998

At the Chapel of Reconciliation, Walsingham, on the occasion of the 50th Anniversary of the Great Cross Carrying Pilgrimage of Prayer and Penance for Peace.

When in 1948 some 400 people walked 200 or more miles carrying heavy crosses in pilgrimage to this holy place, we hoped to see the end of war and the gift of real peace.

It was an occasion of fervent prayer and very real penance - an evident act of faith and a great public demonstration of Christian belief.

But even as we walked, a major war-time ally was changing into a most dangerous enemy, the Cold War had begun and conflicts were already raging in Palestine and elsewhere. As they multiplied and spread we were to witness 50 years filled with ceaseless wars in every part of the world - untold suffering, countless deaths and casualties, terrible atrocities even exceeding those of the World War.

And those 50 years were also to see, by far, the greatest technological advances ever made and an immense increase in wealth in some countries while others sank into even greater poverty.

At the same time there was a major decline in faith in the wealthy countries, the churches have emptied while the shopping malls have filled, family life has disintegrated and selfish pleasure have held sway.

Were our efforts then all in vain? No, by no means. They were all the more necessary and remain even more so today.

Prayers and penance are Our Lady's constant theme in her various apparitions - re-echoed by the Pope. And more amazing events have been achieved which have taken the world largely by surprise: the end of the Cold War, the fall of the Berlin Wall and the collapse of Communism, the peaceful end of apartheid in South Africa; the removal of other tyrannical regimes. Only in heaven will we discover just what an essential part prayer and penance played in these amazing events.

At the same time the Church has been blessed with one of the greatest outpourings of the Holy Spirit since the day of Pentecost. The Second Vatican Council was without doubt the most fruitful in the Church's history and its enrichment of Christian life has got to be fully felt. Relations with our fellow Christians - and other faiths - have been revolutionised, and we have moved from a religion of obligation and fear to one of warmth and love, enriched by the Holy Spirit. We begin to realise how much God loves each one of us; how free and total is his forgiveness and how powerful the Holy Spirit can be in our lives.

There are fewer people in church, but those who are, want to be there and lay people are at last discussing their true role in the church - not as a substitute for a lack of priests - but their rightful place with their immense and varied gifts recognised, and increasingly enriching the life of the community. The Focolare, the Cursillo, the Charismatic Renewal and other lay movements are just examples of what can be achieved by those who really believe, and pray and practice penance.

The Church is still going through a period of purification with much need for repentance of past and present mistakes, sins and scandals - but there are also great signs of hope.

If we are to play our full part in the future, we need to realise as never before the sheer wonder of what God has done for us - how immensely blessed we are.

We are privileged to know "the salvation which you have professed for all the nations to see, a light to enlighten the pagans and the glory of your people Israel."

Simeon saw it and was fully satisfied as he said: "Now, Master, you can let your servant go in peace."

There is nothing more important than to know Jesus Christ, to know him as a friend and for "his message in all its richness to make its home in us."

And yet the future is even better: we look forward to the new Jerusalem, about which Revelation tells us:

"Here God lives among men. He will make his home among them; they shall be his people, and he will be their God …. there will be no more death, and no more mourning or sadness."

The way there is clear - nothing less than the wisdom of God made known to us. Not arbitrary opinions but the very way the world is made and we are designed to relate to it and to each other - all revealed to us in the commandments and the teaching of Jesus. As our first reading put it:

"Whoever listens to me will never have to blush, whoever acts as I dictate will never sin."

It is the greatest folly to ignore the Lord's words. We have a wonderful message - the greatest in the world. We should do all we can to proclaim it as never before - to share with others the hope, the joy, the peace we have come to know - the sure hope of salvation offered free to everyone.

But let us never return to the days of triumphalism. Jesus never promised us a tidy triumph - nor did he achieve one himself. How rightly Simeon proclaimed "He is destined for the fall and the rising of many in Israel, destined to be a sign that is rejected."

We will never succeed in evangelising others without much prayer and penance. We must mend our own hearts before we can touch others. And that means accepting patiently and joyfully the trials and sufferings that come to us far more then taking on chosen penances. To be an active Christian is costly - it was for Mary as Simeon told her "A sword will pierce your own soul too."

She is our model of complete trust, total fidelity and unlimited generous response to whatever God asks.

If we follow Mary in that, we shall come to share her glory in heaven - and that is the purpose of life.

The New Dawn Conference, Wednesday 5th August 1998.

The New Dawn Conference, Shrine Mass, Thursday 6th August 1998.

CATHOLIC PICTORIAL
FRIDAY 14TH AUGUST 1998

New Dawn arrives at Ancient Shrine

-

By CANON JIMMY COLLINS

I was helping with the distribution of Holy Communion when suddenly I noticed the name tags. We all had name tags because this was the New Dawn Conference 1998, but these were different. They were in Russian, and someone had written, under the surname "Russia". I had never before given Holy Communion to a Russian. But they were there, part of the near 3,000 participants. One of them had been baptised the night before and received his Confirmation and First Communion. I know this because it was announced at this Mass, celebrated in the grounds of the ancient Priory.

The grass was green velvet, the sky blue cloak over us and the wonderful Norman (sic) archway, relic of the majestic priory church, stood looking down on us, tolerant of our smallness. We had walked from the tented village at the Catholic shrine, saying the fifteen decades as we wound in the hot sun across the golden countryside. Walsingham was looking at its best. It needed to. There were Czechs and Portuguese, Italians, Irish and Scots. This extraordinary place was coming into its own, as it did when medieval Europe beat a path to its door.

Community

Yet there was not a single signpost on the road to it, except the one outside Fakenham. No mention of it in the brochures kept in the hotels, boarding houses, B & Bs in Norfolk. With curiosity I looked through the Catholic papers this weekend. It was featured in the Pictorial, but not elsewhere. So its silent steady expansion is significant.

Myles Dempsey, the inspiration behind New Dawn, is a gentle, soft spoken individual with the trace of an Irish accent. He walks with a stoop due to arthritic hips, and vascular trouble in the legs. Married with three grown up children, he and his wife Joan were members of a prayer group which met in their home in New Eltham. Out of this prayer group grew the Prince of Peace Community.

This community which has a small core who live residentially, are based at St. Joseph's, a former convent near Baldock in Herts. Myles now has a full time ministry in the Church. He travels a good deal, giving talks and retreats, and has a powerful healing ministry.

His community run three large weekly prayer meetings. The decision to set up New Dawn at Walsingham came during a period of prolonged prayer and discernment. This is the twelfth year and the cost of providing the tents, marquees, Youth Camps, Children's quarters, feeding facilities and so on is in the region of £150,000.

Previously the organisers charged a small fee. This year, because Myles said it must be a venture in faith, no fees were charged and it was left to people's generosity. All through the entire nights of the conference volunteers prayed before the Blessed Sacrament in the Shrine chapel. During the day and late into the evenings priests sat outside in the field for the Sacrament of Reconciliation. Inside the large marquee the atmosphere of faith was infectious.

Beam

One evening a baby was baptised by .... [Fr. Michael Rear - Parochial Administrator for Walsingham]. After the water of christening had been poured and the baby anointed and dressed in a white cloth, the priest held up the tiny bundle of white in both hands with his arms extended above his head. Caught in a beam of light it looked like a white Host. An awed silence fell on the crowded marquee. "Behold a Saint of God", said the priest.

That evening I walked back alone, by the light of a full harvest moon, along the old railway track, to the village. It winds among the wheatfields high above the Holy Mile. The air was warm, scented by the wild flowers along the track. In the village the pilgrims were relaxing around tables outside the Bull and the Black Lion, as men and women had done for nearly a thousand years. Except that is for the dark centuries when a bitter king pulled down the Priory and burnt the statue of Mary of Walsingham, and the vandals had hacked the heads off the statues. But that night there was an all pervading sense of her presence. We knew she was back.

The New Dawn Procession on the 'Old Railway' Path.

The New Dawn Youth Camp Participants.

The Opening Concert of the Centenary Music Festival.
Friday 12th September 1997 - Cambridge Voices, directed by Ian Moore.

Fakenham Choral Society, directed by Graham Hoskins.

The Centenary Music Festival

An appreciation by Nigel Kerry, the Centenary Artistic Director

It is difficult to imagine a celebration without the presence of music to bring it to life. This is especially true in the case of an anniversary. Music seems to own a mysterious quality capable of evoking poignant moments from the past, articulating the mood of the present, while bestowing on the listener a vision and confidence for the future.

It is often said that "Methodism was born in song." But just as Wesley was, no doubt, encouraged and befriended by music on many a long and arduous journey, so too were the thousands of pilgrims in medieval times whose footsteps were quickened by singing the praises of their Lord and His Mother as they walked, trudged and hobbled no doubt to their intended destination. In Walsingham today, the still countryside enveloping the Shrine, continues to sound with the songs of the pilgrims as they, like their brothers and sisters of old, journey towards this place, which for them is both sign and foretaste of their true homeland.

It seemed entirely fitting, then, that the celebrations marking the restoration of pilgrimage to Walsingham should have a strong musical element. This music was not just confined to the many solemn liturgies that occurred during the year, but was broadened to include a concert series that would appeal to a wider constituency. Throughout the festival we were fortunate to welcome to the Shrine many people from the immediate locality and around the county, as well as those tourists and occasional visitors who were attracted by the musicians we had assembled and the music we had programmed. In this way we welcomed people to the Shrine, many of whom were from different Christian traditions, or different faiths, or no faith at all. Clearly those who attended the concerts were warm in their praise of what they had heard. But through this musical hospitality offered by the Shrine during the year, who knows what seeds of faith were sown in hearts and minds?

So it was that from September 1997 to September 1998 over 650 musicians, many of international distinction, made the journey to the Shrine. Naturally, a good deal of choral music was programmed, written to accompany many varying Marian texts. Indeed by the time we had reached the last work of the last concert, over 350 anthems and motets - ancient and modern - dedicated to Our Lady had been performed, by composers from many different countries.

The opening and closing concerts were both headed with the titles of two Marian antiphons regularly heard at the Shrine - 'Salve Regina' and 'Regina Coeli'. To launch the festival we welcomed one of the country's most innovative and versatile chamber choirs, 'Cambridge Voices' directed by their irrepressible conductor Ian Moore. Their programme ranged from a version of the Salve Regina by the 15th century English composer Robert Wylkinson, to the first performance in this country of a new work by the contemporary Swiss composer, Carl Rütti. He took as his text, the ancient and beautiful office hymn to Our Lady, 'Ave Maris Stella' - 'Hail, Star of the Ocean'.

To complete the weekend festivities, the next evening saw a powerful and moving one-man performance by the actor Patrick McGrady of Milton's 'Paradise Lost'. The audience included a number of sixth form students grateful for the opportunity to witness an arid 'A' level text being brought to life before their eyes!

Walsingham and its Shrine clearly has an important place in the historical and religious fabric of our country. This is, of course, just as true of the county of Norfolk where the Shrine is located. It was for this reason that the authorities of the Norfolk and Norwich Festival approached the Shrine to see whether it would be possible to promote a concert as part of the Centenary celebrations. So in October we welcomed the Schidlof String Quartet (who in 1997 were quartet-in-residence at the Norfolk and Norwich Festival) who performed a programme of Haydn, Brahms, and Janacek. They were also joined in this concert by the celebrated cellist, Anthony Pleeth, and violist, Yoko Inove.

The last of the three concerts in 1997 was given by the King's Lynn Chorus. Walsingham's links with this town are strong, and well documented elsewhere in this book. So it was fitting then that this choir, which was born of the famous King's Lynn Festival, should visit the Shrine during the Centenary. Moreover, their Director, John Jordan also happens to be Director of Music at the Shrine. Their concert fell on St. Cecilia's day, the Patron Saint of Musicians, and their performance included a wide range of musical styles from Palestrina and Byrd through to Schubert and Mendelssohn.

To conclude the musical year at the Shrine, the now annual Advent Carol Service 'In Joyful Hope' took place on Gaudete Sunday. This is a very popular service in the village calendar, the music being led by the augmented choir of the Shrine. After the heady opening months of the festival, we took the opportunity offered by the bleakness of a Norfolk winter, to have a rest and prepare ourselves for the next stage of the festival.

Many of the musical highlights that characterised the celebrations took part, quite appropriately, in the context of the Sacred Liturgy. This was particularly the case when we welcomed the choirs from three of East Anglia's cathedral churches that have monastic roots. On Ash Wednesday, the Choir of Peterborough Cathedral, with their Vice-Dean and Precentor joined the Shrine community for Mass, singing some of the finest polyphonic music written for the Lenten season by Lassus, Tallis and Byrd.

Then in March, we celebrated the Patronal Feast of the Shrine, the Annunciation of Our Lord to the Blessed Virgin Mary. To mark also the beginning of the Historical Conference that week, a special concert was programmed. The Thames Chamber Orchestra under their Director Keith Marshall, comprises some of London's most experienced and talented players. They launched the week in fine and impressive style with a colourful programme which included music by Handel, Mozart and Huw Spratling, a composer with many links to Walsingham, who now lives in Norfolk.

For the Feastday itself the Solemn Mass offered by Bishop Smith of East Anglia, was sung by the Choir of our sister cathedral in Norwich. This in itself was a unique ecumenical occasion for Walsingham, and we were delighted that the choir made the journey with the Archdeacon of Norwich. The setting for the Mass they chose was a contemporary one written by Malcolm Archer for the 900th anniversary of the foundation of the cathedral.

One aspect of the festival which was particularly exciting was our good fortune in having a 'composer in residence'. Paul Johnson is a composer, himself a Catholic, living and working in King's Lynn. We were delighted that during the year many of his sacred works were performed and some premiered at the Shrine. Most notably 'The Centenary Mass' which was performed as part of the opening celebrations and at Westminster Cathedral later in the year. In April he presented (with the aid of a new choir he formed for the occasion called Eastern Voices), a somewhat tongue-in-cheek programme of music and readings called 'The Church Observ'd'. The evening served as a gentle, polite reminder to us of the pitfalls and hazards of too much churchiness! But at the same time, the evening also evoked a devotional spirit as we heard for the first time Paul's tender anthem to the Blessed Sacrament - 'Corpus Christi the Fountainhead'.

In May, one of the major events of the year took place - The Festival of Flowers. The opening Mass was a splendid and uplifting occasion, the music being provided by the professional choir from one of London's most famous Catholic Churches - the Jesuit Church in Farm Street, Mayfair. In the evening, the Farm Street Singers were joined by the well known actress from stage, screen and radio, Liza Goddard. In the beautiful surroundings of the Anglican Parish Church of St. Mary in Walsingham, made all the more resplendent by the floral arrangements, they performed for us music and readings for the Church's year. The music, poetry and prose led us from Advent and Christmas, to Lent, Easter, Ascension and Pentecost, finishing with Our Lady's Assumption. Music by Gabrieli, Duruflé, and Paul Johnson, was complemented by readings from Blake, Wordsworth and Newman.

Then to celebrate the Feast of Pentecost at the end of May, the second local choral society in the area, this time from nearby Fakenham were joined by a large orchestra to perform Haydn's grand oratorio 'The Creation'. It is a particular joy that this enthusiastic choir are now visiting the Shrine on a regular basis to perform many large scale sacred works.

Moving into June, we celebrated with the whole Church the ancient Feast of Corpus Christi with Forty Hours of Adoration and Thanksgiving. During this time, a Holy Hour contained the performance of St. Thomas Aquinas's Sequence 'Lauda Sion' set to music by Mendelssohn. This was performed by members of the King's Lynn Chorus and St. Margaret's Church directed by John Jordan. The Solemn Mass next day was sung by the boys from Ely Cathedral Choir directed by Paul Trepte who was also the composer of the powerful and moving Mass setting.

Friday 28th August 1998 - The New London Consort, directed by Philip Pickett

Monday 7th September 1998 - The Erard Ensemble.

Tuesday 8th September 1998 - The Curate's Egg, directed by Adey Grummet.

Wednesday 9th September 1998 - The Maggini String Quartet.

140

At the end of June the talented new chamber ensemble, Kontrabande, founded and directed by Charles Humphries, presented a moving programme of music by J. S. Bach. In July, two more premieres of songs by Paul Johnson were given by the Australian soprano Adey Grummet, while in August the acclaimed New London Consort, artists-in-residence at London's South Bank Centre, performed a strangely mesmeric concert of music to Our Lady by the 13th century French monk, Gautier de Coincy.

The Centenary Celebrations concluded in September 1998. The occasion was marked by a week of Solemn Liturgies and concerts of superlative standard. To open the week the young players who make up 'The Erard Ensemble' delighted us with their sparkling interpretations of Brahms, Mozart, Debussy and Ravel.

The next evening concert was called 'The Lily that Dazzles' and was given by the glittering all female professional choir 'The Curate's Egg'. They performed this concert by candlelight and for many who attended, this was undoubtedly one of the most moving concerts of the whole year. The choral music was chosen in honour of Our Lady, whose birthday was being celebrated by the Church on that day. Included in the performance was the world premiere of a haunting and dramatic new work, 'Shimmering Glimmering', by a former BBC Young Composer of the Year, Lynne Plowman.

The next day we welcomed four good friends of the Shrine, the Maggini String Quartet, who were visiting us for the third time in their own 10th anniversary year. They played quite brilliantly, to a hushed audience, music by Haydn, Elgar and Tchaikovsky. On Thursday of Festival Week, former choral scholars of Cambridge University called 'Henry's Eight' presented a varied programme of sacred music by composers such as Byrd, Tallis, Poulenc and Henry VIII!

The final two concerts brought to the Shrine, quite rightly, artists of world renown. On the Friday night, the award winning Norwegian trumpeter, Ole Edvard Antonsen, was joined by one of the finest organists of his generation, Wayne Marshall. They presented a breathtakingly colourful, joyful and exuberant programme of music which called forth two encores from the large audience.

Then exactly a year after the Centenary Festival of Music had begun we had arrived at the final concert. When asked to direct this festival, there was no doubt in my mind who should be invited to give the final concert. Now established as one of the finest choirs in the world, I was delighted and moved when James O'Donnell, Master of Music at Westminster Cathedral, said how 'honoured' he and his choir were in being invited to sing the final concert.

Those fortunate people who could get a ticket (the concert predictably sold out some time before) were not to be disappointed. Some of the most beautiful music ever written for the Mother of God by composers from the 15th century to our own day was performed. The music was sung with the utmost precision, passion and devotion, confirming what so many in the musical world have to say about this choir: that in their daily praise of the Creator they are surely one of the glories of the Catholic Church in this land.

For their encore, no intricate music, instead the congregation were invited to rise and join them in singing that beautiful prayer to Our Lady offered at the Shrine day in and day out - Salve Regina. Surely the most appropriate anthem to sing as we stood to give thanks for what had passed and looked out to the future in joyful hope.

Before the festival began, I was asked to write some words of introduction, explaining why we were having a music festival as part of the Centenary Celebrations. These words I offer again, as I believe that throughout this year we have been fortunate to experience in so many wonderful ways, through this offering of music, our God who created it and causes it to flower - He it is who has been gracious to us and blessed us.

'This festival is not simply about a special series of concerts. Every spontaneous note of hymnody of song raised on the Holy Mile, to the sumptuous sounds of the finest choirs, are all part and parcel of the Centenary Year celebrations.

It all promises to be quite a party, and yes, we have allowed ourselves to be a little extravagant. But, if anyone should ask why 'the perfume is being thus wasted', one of England's greatest sons, who has nurtured an abiding tender love for Mary, provides us with a characteristically wise answer; reminding us that for the Church, music must never be viewed as a dispensable nicety, rather-

"Music is the expression of ideas greater and more profound than any in the visible world, ideas which centre, indeed, in Him whom Catholicism manifests, who is the seat of all beauty, order and perfection whatever."'

The Venerable John Henry Cardinal Newman.

-

Nigel Kerry was formerly Director of Music at the National Shrine, and Artistic Director of the Centenary Music Festival.

In April 1998 he was appointed Organist and Director of Music of the Church of Our Lady of the Assumption and the English Martyrs, Cambridge.

The Music of Paul Johnson, including
The Centenary Mass Setting
is available on
CD or Tape from the Slipper Chapel Bookshop
01328 820495

The recording, entitled "The Prioress In Spring", is by
Cambridge Voices, Adey Grummet, Charlie Humphries and
Nigel Kerry, all of whom gave performances at the Shrine
during the Centenary Music Festival.

The Final Concert - Saturday 12th September 1998, Westminster Cathedral Choir, directed by James O'Donnell.

Paul Johnson (Composer in Residence), John Joubert (Composer, Six Short Preludes on English Hymn tunes), Nigel Kerry (Centenary Artistic Director) and Adey Grummet, Friday 31st July 1998 "The Song Ascending."

-

Special week to mark milestone

-

A week of special events culminating in a visit from a leading religious figure will mark an important milestone at Walsingham.

Cardinal Basil Hume, the Archbishop of Westminster, will participate in the Dowry of Mary Pilgrimage on Sunday September 13th, as part of the Centenary Celebrations at the Roman Catholic Shrine.

He will be joined by the Bishop of East Anglia, the Rt. Rev Peter Smith, for the pilgrimage which begins at 1 p.m.

It will be the final event in a week-long programme of activities at the Chapel of Reconciliation at the village's [R. C.] Shrine of Our Lady at 7.30 p.m. nightly to mark 100 years of modern pilgrimage to the village.

Other highlights of the programme include a concert by the Erard Ensemble on Monday, a choir of female professional singers from London [The Curates Egg] performing a range of music the following evening at the same time, and the Maggini String Quartet performing works by Haydn, Elgar and Tchaikovsky on Wednesday.

Then a group of former Cambridge scholars [Henry's Eight] will present a concert of sacred and secular music from Byrd to The Beatles on Thursday, organist Wayne Marshall and trumpeter Ole Antonsen will perform music by a range of composers next Friday and the Westminster Cathedral choir makes its first visit to the shrine the following evening for a concert, which will be followed by a grand fireworks display.

Dom Charles Fitzgerald Lombard OSB.

HOMILY PREACHED BY
DOM. CHARLES FITZGERALD-LOMBARD, TITULAR ABBOT OF
GLASTONBURY, FORMER ABBOT OF DOWNSIDE AND
PATRON OF THE CENTENARY CELEBRATIONS
Tuesday 8th September 1998

At the Chapel of Reconciliation on the Feast of the Birthday of the Blessed Virgin Mary during the Centenary Festival Week.

I think most of you know that the normal day on which the feast of a saint is celebrated is the anniversary of the saint's death on earth which is, of course, the anniversary also of his or her birth into the new life of heaven. But there are three very notable cases where the physical birth of a child into our world was of such exceptional significance in the story of our redemption that their birthday or nativity is celebrated as a major feast of the church. The most celebrated of these is, of course, Christmas Day - the birthday of Our Lord Jesus Christ, then there is the Birth of John the Baptist to Our Lady's cousin Elizabeth which was announced as a part of the message of salvation by the angel Gabriel and finally we have today's feast day - the birth of the Immaculate Mother of our God, the beginning of the visible story. In all three cases we do not know the actual date of either birth or death but that is of no real consequence. We know enough from the scriptures and we are able to add enough from traditions going back to the earliest years of the Church to be able to tell a coherent story. Among those traditions are some that are so strong that they have come to form a part of the *consensus fidelium*, the common faith that we share. I am thinking here in particular of Mary's Immaculate Conception and Assumption, of the Church's teaching that it is surely unfitting that the soul of the Mother of God should have been stained by original sin or that her body should have become corrupt after death and that she was therefore privileged to experience before any of us the mysterious transformation which we refer to in the Creed as The Resurrection of the Body as well as the Soul into its heavenly state.

As with so many articles of our faith, we westerners who have minds drilled in the disciplines of logic, rationalism and the exact sciences, have to remind ourselves that it is out of the human spirit, inspired by the Divine or Holy Spirit, that we receive and enjoy our less rational but higher faculties of humanity - love, music, poetry and faith (to name a few) and that it is only with this eye of the heart that we can trust and accept the truths of our faith and, indeed, the existence of God himself.

What can I say to you that will summarize the meeting of so many great signs? How can we all respond to these events in a way that lifts them out of empty ritual and gives them a meaning and a message for our everyday lives? I think we all, in our different ways, find ourselves bewildered by the conflicting pressures of modern life, and yet as Christians we all know that peace is to be found in fidelity to our convictions. That fidelity is something that we fortify by prayer, by keeping in touch with the God who loves us, in the same way that any relationship is strengthened and maintained by communication. In this we have the outstanding example of the Saints, even though we ourselves hardly aspire to that rank. But let us suppose that we simply stand before God as one of the great hoard of unsung heroes: sinners, but not spectacularly so, right minded and faithful in our religious duties, but not exactly saints. "What is man," says the psalmist, "that God should be mindful of him," and, as if reflecting that, Elizabeth says as you will remember from the Christmas story: "Who am I that the mother of my Lord should visit me." But, in his merciful plan for our salvation, God has given us other routes to himself, more homely and less awesome personalities than the Almighty Father and his Holy Spirit on whom we may focus our affections: pre-eminently he has given us his own Divine Son, our Lord and Saviour Jesus Christ, true God yet approachable as true man; and Mary his Blessed Mother; and indeed any one of the saints.

From the earliest times and, significantly, in the Eastern and more devotional tradition of God's Church, Our Blessed Lady has held a unique position in the devotional life of Catholic Christendom, not only because of her approachability as our spiritual mother, but also because of her unique position among the saints as one chosen out of the whole of humanity. For what other saint had the power to say 'yes' or 'no' to the offer of a Saviour for the whole world; what other saint, what other woman, was thus overshadowed by the Spirit of God himself; what other member of our fallen race could hold the title of Theotokos, the Mother of her own God.

Recent years have witnessed a striking change in Catholic attitude towards Mary. Seeing Our Lady from a perspective of true and defensible theology, free of excess, yet recognizing her unique position, is the key to true and fruitful devotion. This point was well made during the Second Vatican Council when there was something of a crisis, as hot debate developed over whether Our Lady should be the subject of a special document as had been planned or whether the chapter on her should be incorporated into the document on the Church: our own Abbot Butler was partly responsible for persuading the Council Fathers of the importance of seeing Mary primarily in the context of the Church so that we could see her in her true role as Mother of the Church, Mother of all Christians, Mother of God. Thus we are encouraged to honour her today as an image of the Church, spotless, immaculate.

There is a wonderful passage in the revised Council document which gives us a vision of what the Mother of God should mean to us:

> "The Blessed Virgin was eternally predestined to be the Mother of God - By decree of Divine providence, she served on earth as the mother of our Redeemer. She conceived, brought forth and nourished Christ, presented him to the Father in the temple and was united with him in suffering as he died on the cross. In a very special way she co-operated in the Saviour's work of restoring supernatural life to the human race. For this reason she is a mother to us, the Church, in the order of grace."

We pray today, here at Walsingham, that the grace of Almighty God and the intercession of Our Lady, Saint Benedict and all the Saints may bring peace, happiness and salvation to all of us in these troubled times. Amen.

His Eminence Cardinal George Basil Hume OSB, Archbishop of Wesminster.

HOMILY PREACHED BY
H. E. CARDINAL GEORGE BASIL HUME
ARCHBISHOP OF WESTMINSTER.
At the Chapel of Reconciliation during the Dowry of Mary Pilgrimage Mass
closing the Centenary Celebrations
Sunday 13th September 1998

In our family, celebrating the Feast of the Assumption, a long time before the war, was a very special day. No holiday clothes that day - a special lunch and, of course, attendance at Mass. And those childhood, teenage memories, they remain and the Feast of the Assumption has remained an important date in our family, and, indeed, in the family which is the church.

This year it was different, and we were not thinking so much how Our Lady followed her son into heaven, but we were thinking of her rather, standing at the foot of the cross. Because on August the 15th, our minds and our hearts were choked, were they not, with the events that took place in Omagh and not long before that Nairobi, and Dar-es-Salam.

The appropriate thoughts were of Our Lady standing at the foot of the cross as she watched her beloved son suffering, dying. And as we watched with her, standing with her at the foot of the cross, sharing the pain and suffering of so many people, we listen, surely, with her to the words spoken by Him, the precious words of a dying man. His wish to forgive, his wish to have us with Him in paradise, "this day you will be with me in paradise". His wish to express his love for each one of us. "I thirst", He thirsts with each one of us and He thirsts for me. To forgive, to give hope, to love - those precious gifts which our Lord has given us.

Then if one went on standing next to Our Blessed Lady at the foot of the Cross, thinking of all those people throughout the world, suffering for one reason or another, and heard our Lord praying the psalm "My God, my God. Why have you forsaken me?" Surely that prayer of Our Lord has been echoed down the ages and so often why, why, why?

And then, we remember how he prayed that other psalm. "Into your hands, Lord, I commend my spirit." Whatever the darkness, whatever the tragedy, whatever the pain. "Into your hands, Lord, I commend my spirit." Abandonment to the will of God. "Trust in his plans for us, certain of his love for us."

However bleak, however dark, those words - "Into your hands, Lord, I commend my spirit" we echoed them, did we not, a moment ago when we prayed, "Here I am Lord, I am coming to do your will." Abandonment to the will of God.

We stood with Our Lady at the foot of the Cross. And she always points to Him, she always urges us to listen to Him and in our day this is especially important. We remember how on one occasion, going into the synagogue, as was His custom, He read from the Prophet Isaiah "the spirit of the Lord is upon Me, has anointed Me to bring good news to the poor, to bring sight to the blind, set captives free and declare the Lord's year of favour."

The jubilee which Walsingham has been celebrating is, surely, in some manner a preparation for the Great Jubilee, the great Holy Year, and as we prepare Our Lady is present, urging us to listen to Our Lord and to watch him.

Can you remember how in that moment in the synagogue, we read how He rolled up the scroll, handed it to an attendant and then we read, "all eyes in the synagogue were fixed on Him"? And it seems to me that, that Gospel passage from St. Luke, which I have just quoted, is a kind of charter for our celebration of our Holy Year. And therefore meditating on it and reflecting on it must be part of our preparation to celebrate the Holy Year, the Great Jubilee. But the key to the whole thing - that all our eyes should be fixed on him and I think that this is Our Lady's message to us - keep your eyes fixed on Him, my Son, true God and true man because the Millennium, the Holy Year or the Great Jubilee as we call it, will make no sense unless our eyes are fixed on Him. You will recall how at the marriage Feast at Cana, Our Lady turned to those waiters, when the wine had run out, and she said, "Do whatever He tells you". And His mother, our Mother too, "Woman, behold your son, Son behold your Mother" words addressed to each one of us. And she, our Mother, as I would think, is saying to us, keep your eyes fixed on Him, Jesus Christ, true God and true man. Listen to his word, discover Him in the Blessed Sacrament on the altar and then that other thing she says to us "Do whatever he tells you"

And so when we come to one of her shrines as people have been coming here these last hundred years, we listen to her speaking to us, keep our eyes on Him, listen, listen and do whatever he tells us. God bless you, God keep you dry.

152

The Dowry of Mary Procession, Sunday 13th September 1998.

Rt Rev Peter Smith, LLB, JCD, Bishop of East Anglia.

HOMILY PREACHED BY
THE RT. REV. PETER SMITH LLB, JCD,
BISHOP OF EAST ANGLIA
Sunday 13th September 1998

In Walsingham Abbey Grounds, during the Dowry of Mary Pilgrimage, marking the closing of the Centenary Celebrations.

(On the text: John 17:11-19 - 'That they may be one like us'.)

Jesus the 'man for others', prays at the Last Supper, for his disciples both present and future. He prays for them for three reasons:

i. Because his disciples belong to the Father, and everything and everyone who belongs to the Father belongs to him and is precious to him;

ii. Secondly, he prays for his disciples because they share in the life and love of Jesus and acknowledge him in faith for who he is;

iii. Thirdly, because he is soon to leave them and he is concerned for the welfare and well-being of those who have already and will in the future profess their belief in him.

In essence, Jesus is saying to his heavenly Father: "I, your only-begotten Son, am praying for these here present, and for those who are to come, who will believe in my name, and believe that it was you who sent me into the world to forgive sins and reconcile the whole world to you."

But Jesus prays particularly for one special gift - the gift of communion, the gift of unity, the gift of a life of intimacy with himself and his heavenly Father. His prayer is that his disciples through the ages will remain in a communion of life and love through faith, so that all may be one in God, Father, Son and Spirit.

It is this communion with the Father and the Son through the gift of the Spirit which makes us holy and which is a necessary condition for us, as the disciples of Jesus, to carry out the mission he has entrusted to us - to prolong and make real in our own times the mission of Jesus himself. That mission is to draw all people to himself, and through him, with him and in him, to draw all people to the Father in the unity of the Holy Spirit.

The loving obedience of Jesus and his communion of life and love with his Father is the model for all disciples in every age. In baptism we are given the gift of the Spirit and so enter into a life-giving communion with the living God through lives of faith, hope and love. And this communion of life and love through the power of the Holy Spirit who dwells in us is also the source and cause of our communion with each other as members of Christ's body, the Church.

That communion, that oneness, that intimacy is not simply and solely an interior and spiritual communion and oneness, but is manifested, lived out, concretely and visibly in the communion of the Church - the visible body of Christ, the community of faith. And we know that we "are in full communion with the Catholic Church here on earth when we are joined with Christ in his visible body, through the profession of faith, the sacraments and ecclesiastical governance."

In responding to the prayer of Jesus, we too pray this afternoon in the presence of the Blessed Sacrament, for the grace to maintain, strengthen and extend that communion for which Christ prayed. Let us pray for the grace never to do anything which might harm that communion for which Christ prayed; let us pray for the grace to foster that communion through our communion with the Bishops, and through them our communion with the whole College of Bishops throughout the world who are in communion with the Bishop of Rome, the Pope.

The Sanctuary of the Anglican Shrine during the Festival of Flowers, 22nd - 25th May 1998.

Bishop Peter Smith, Councillor and Mrs Clifford Walters (the 1997 Mayor and Mayoress of the Borough of King's Lynn and West Norfolk), Cardinal Cahal Daly and Dr. Paul Richards, the 1998 Mayor of King's Lynn and West Norfolk in the Red Mount Chapel, Tuesday 19th August 1997 at the opening of the Centenary Celebrations.

EASTERN DAILY PRESS
MONDAY SEPTEMBER 14th 1998

-

Catholics Celebrate Pilgrimage

-

Cardinal Basil Hume was among about 2000 people marking the end of the celebration of 100 years of pilgrimage to the Roman Catholic National Shrine at Walsingham yesterday.

The Archbishop of Westminster preached during the Holy Mass at the shrine.

He then joined a procession along the holy mile for prayers and Benediction of the [Blessed] Sacrament at the Priory Grounds, which is the site of the original shrine.

Tens of thousands of people have visited Walsingham - dubbed England's Nazareth - during the year, which has marked the centenary of modern day pilgrimage.

It was on August 20th 1897 that the first post Reformation pilgrims returned to Walsingham since its destruction in 1538.

The Director of the National Shrine, Father Alan Williams, said: "It has been a very busy centenary year and a very good year. Numbers of visitors are up and today is very special for us." Other people taking part in the Dowry of Mary Pilgrimage yesterday were the Rt. Rev Peter Smith, Bishop of East Anglia and King's Lynn and West Norfolk Borough Mayor, [Dr.] Paul Richards. During the past week there has been a music festival as part of the centenary celebrations, which has featured many groups including the Choir of Westminster Cathedral.

-

Pope's Message for Walsingham Centenary

-

Hundreds of Roman Catholic pilgrims came to Walsingham last Sunday as the Centenary celebrations of the founding of their Shrine came to a close.

Visitors who had travelled from all over Britain - and some from overseas - gathered for the Dowry of Mary Pilgrimage, which was jointly led by the head of the Roman Catholic Church in Britain, Cardinal Basil Hume, and Bishop of East Anglia, the Right Reverend Peter Smith.

The day's celebrations began with Mass at the Chapel of Reconciliation and a procession, along the Holy Mile, to the Priory grounds in Walsingham village for prayers at the site of the original shrine.

Father Alan Williams, head of the Roman Catholic Shrine, read out the original letter from Pope John Paul II in praise and encouragement for the year of Centenary celebration.

In the programme The Pope added: "When Catholic pilgrims returned to Walsingham in 1897 they could have had little idea of the great developments that would follow over the next 100 years. More and more people of goodwill, and of various Christian denominations are now making their way to "England's Nazareth" in their search for God under the patronage of Our Lady of Walsingham. It is my prayer that God's work in Walsingham over the next 100 years will once again surpass our greatest hopes and desires."

The Shrine was set up by the then Lady of the Manor of Little Walsingham, Richeldis de Favarches, in 1061. Tradition says that she was told in a vision to create England's Nazareth at Walsingham.

The Priory and shrine were destroyed in 1538 and the Statue of Our Lady taken to London and publicly destroyed. The shrine lay almost forgotten until interest was rekindled in the late 19th century. The first pilgrimage since the Reformation took place on August 20th, 1897.

Leading it was a new statue which was brought from London to Lynn by train with parishioners then taking it to Walsingham. To mark the event Borough Mayor, Dr. Paul Richards, took part in the final day celebrations and joined the procession where Lynn parishioners once more carried the statue.

Cardinal Hume greeting Revd Martin Warner, Administrator of the Anglican Shrine.

Appendix I
SHRINE CENTENARY DIARY

AUGUST 1997

19 Opening Mass, Red Mount King's Lynn (**Bishop Smith**)
    Guild of Our Lady of Ransom process with Replica Statue to
    Massingham St. Mary
    Guild of Our Lady of Ransom Centenary Dinner
20 Solemn Mass of Welcome for the King's Lynn Replica Statue
    (**Cardinal Daly**)
    Centenary Window unveiled followed by procession to the Abbey
    Grounds for prayers and Benediction
    Evening Party at Shrine (Jazz Orchestra) Fireworks
23 National Walsingham Association and Guild of Our Lady of Ransom.
    (**Bishop K. O'Brien**)
31 National Catenian (**Bishop Tripp**)

SEPTEMBER

6   Leeds Diocese (**Bishop Konstant**)
6/7   Liverpool Archdiocese
7   Legion of Mary (**Bishop Nichols**)
12   *"Salve Regina", Music in Honour of the Blessed Virgin,*
        Cambridge Voices
13   Knights of St. Columba (**Bishop Pargeter**)
13   *"Paradise Lost" - Patrick McGrady*
14   Dowry of Mary (**Cardinal Hume, Bishop Smith, Bishop Clark**)
20   Guild of Our Lady of Ransom Walkers arrive Walsingham
21   LIFE
27   Faith and Light
27   Catholic Police Guild
27/28   Middlesborough Diocese (**Bishop Crowley**)

OCTOBER

4   Walsingham Association East Anglian Federation
11   Ecumenical Society of the Blessed Virgin Mary,
        Catholic League, and Society of Mary
17   *The Schidlof Quartet*

NOVEMBER

1   *The Singers Company*
4/7   Walsingham Association Retreat
8/9   Walsingham Association, AGM
8   *Mass for Deceased Benefactors. Gresham's Chapel Choir*
22   *"Hail Bright Cecilia" King's Lynn Chorus directed by John Jordan*

DECEMBER

14   *"In Joyful Hope" Advent Carol Service - Shrine Voices with John Jordan*

JANUARY 1998

1   *Mary Mother of God* (**Bishop Clark**)

FEBRUARY

25   *Ash Wednesday, Choir of Peterborough Cathedral*

MARCH

6/8   Walsingham Association Bi-annual Meeting
21   Westminster Cathedral Walsingham Centenary Mass
      (**Apostolic Nuncio Archbishop Pablo Puente, Bishop Rawsthorne, Bishop Clark**)
23/27 Residential Historical Seminar at Elmham House
23   *Thames Chamber Orchestra*
25   *The Annunciation - Solemn Mass with The Choir of Norwich Cathedral*
      (**Bishop Smith**)

APRIL

7   Oscott Seminary
10   Student Cross
16/17 Plymouth Diocese (**Bishop Budd**)
17   *"The Church Observ'd" - Eastern Voices*
19   Divine Mercy
19   Catholic Aids Link

MAY

2	Catholic Men's Society

2   Catholic Men's Society
3   Polish National (**Archbishop Wesoly**)
4   Archconfraternity of St. Stephen (**Bishop Smith**)
9   Birmingham Archdiocese (**Bishop Pargeter**)
16   Deaf
17   Dominican
        Salford Diocese
22/25 Flower Festival
        Opening Mass, Farm Street Choir (**Bishop Clark**)
        "Music in Season"- Farm Street Singers- Liza Goddard
23   Combined Oratories
23/24 Catholic Families' Association
25   THE ANGLICAN NATIONAL PILGRIMAGE
26   East Anglia Diocesan Children's (**Bishop Smith**)
30   Sons of Divine Providence
30   *Haydn's Creation - Fakenham Choral Society*

JUNE

6   Catholic Women's League (**Bishop Walmsley**)
7   Hallam Diocese (**Bishop Clark**)
8   Allen Hall Seminary
9/11   40 Hours Devotion
10   *Mendelssohn's Lauda Sion in Liturgical performance*
11   *Corpus Christi Choir of Ely Cathedral* (**Bishop McCartie**)
13   Brentwood (**Bishop McMahon**)
14   East Anglian Diocese/Knights of Malta (**Bishop Smith**)
15   Primary Schools'
20   Northampton Diocese (**Bishop McCartie**)
21   Birmingham Archdiocese Catholic Handicapped Fellowship
        (**Bishop Pargeter**)
26   *"Bach to Bach" - Kontrabande*
28   Caribbean

JULY

4   Marist
5   S.V.P. Sick (**Bishop Smith**)
6   Union of Catholic Mothers Torchlight Service (**Bishop Brain**)

7	Union of Catholic Mothers (**Bishops Brain and Smith**)
11	Reparation and Consecration (**Bishop Nichols**)
12	"A Day with Mary"
16/17	Cross Carrying 50th Anniversary (**Bishop Griffiths**)
18	Order of Carmelites and Order of Discalced Carmelites.
19	Tamil
	Exhibition at King's Lynn Museum "Pilgrimage" opens
23/24	*A Celebration of Margery Kempe (King's Lynn Festival Event for the Centenary)*
26	St Patrick's Missionary Society (**Bishop Clark**)
31	*"The Song Ascending" - Adey Grummet and Nigel Kerry*

AUGUST

1	Lambeth Conference Visit (**Bishop Clark**)
3-7	New Dawn Conference
8	Centenary Youth Event
9-13	Ecumenical Youth
10	Padre Pio Prayer Groups
14	*Centenary Barbecue - Jazz , Norwich Barbershop and Line Up 'n' Dance*
15	*The Assumption* Ecumenical Procession
19	101st Anniversary of refounded Shrine (**Bishop Griffiths**)
28	*"The Miracles of Mary" - New London Consort*

SEPTEMBER

5	Leeds (**Bishop Konstant**)
5/6	Liverpool
7	*The Erard Ensemble*
8	*Our Lady's Birthday* (**Dom Charles Fitzgerald Lombard**)
	"The Lily That Dazzles" - The Curates Egg
9	*Maggini String Quartet*
10	*Henry's Eight*
11	*"Pulling out the Stops" - Wayne Marshall (organ) and Ole Edvard Antonson (trumpet)*
12	Servites
12	*"Regina Coeli" - Westminster Cathedral Choir*
13	Dowry of Mary Pilgrimage (**Cardinal Hume, Bishop Smith and Bishop Clark**) followed by Procession to Abbey Grounds for prayers and Benediction to close the Centenary Celebrations.

Appendix II
CENTENARY PERSONNEL

Shrine Director	Alan Williams, sm
Box Office Manager	Audrey Broughton
Concert Publicity	Moira Eaglin
Centenary Composer	Paul Johnson
Shrine Director of Music	John Jordan
Centenary Artistic Director	Nigel Kerry
Centenary Co-ordinator	Timothy V McDonald
Pilgrimage Co-ordinator/ Shrine Archivist	Anne Milton
Centenary Photographer	Peter Murray, sm
Centenary Publications	Debbie Parker
Flower Festival Designer	Margaret Peel

CENTENARY COMMITTEE

Fr. Alan Williams	Shrine Director
Mgr. Anthony Stark	Master of the Guild of Our Lady of Ransom
Mgr. Edward McBride	Vicar General
Fr. Anthony Shryane	Parish Priest, King's Lynn
Mr. Dennis Gerrard	Walsingham Association Representative

Appendix III

PHOTOGRAPHIC ACKNOWLEDGEMENTS

The photographs in this publication are reproduced by kind permission of the following:

Father Peter Murray, sm: *pp. 8, 11, 12t, 19b, 20, 21, 23, 24, 25, 27, 28, 31, 32, 39, 40, 43, 44t, 47, 48, 57, 58, 61, 66, 69, 70, 77, 78t, 79, 81, 90, 94, 96, 97t, 98l, 101, 102r, 104, 105, 109, 110, 113, 118, 121b, 122t, 124, 125, 126, 130, 133, 134t, 139, 140, 144, 153, 154, 157, 158, Back Cover.*

Miss Anne Milton: *pp. 12b, 15, 16, 19t, 44b, 65, 78b, 82, 85, 86, 89, 106, 121t, 122b, 150, 161.*

Mrs. Debbie Parker: *Front Cover, pp. 91, 98r, 102l.*

Mr. Timothy McDonald: *pp. 63, 71, 93, 117, 134b.*

Mr. Tom Coleman: *p. 97b.*

John Dove Photography: *pp. 73, 74.*

Mr. Alfred Fisher: *p 62.*

The photographs on pages 114 of the Bishop of Brentwood, and 146 of Dom Charles Fitzgerald Lombard, OSB were kindly provided by Bishop McMahon and Dom Charles respectively.

Acknowledgements

I would like to thank the Editors of the following newspapers who have kindly allowed articles from their publications to be reproduced here: Eastern Daily Press, Lynn News, Dereham and Fakenham Times, The Times, The Telegraph, The Independent, The Catholic Herald, The Catholic Pictorial, Church Building Magazine, West Sussex County Times. The copyright of these articles remains with the various publications.

There are numerous people to thank for their efforts towards the success of the Centenary. This includes the parishioners of Wells and Walsingham, the volunteers who give their time so freely to the Shrine and, of course, there is the staff of the Shrine and Pilgrim Bureau. The staff especially deserve my heart-felt thanks as they bore the brunt of the increased workload. Anne Milton and Audrey Broughton have been tremendously supportive of the Centenary, and I owe a great personal debt to Debbie Parker for her assistance in the arranging of the Centenary calendar, events and programmes, and in particular for her desktop publishing skills in the production of the six books in the Centenary Publications series.

Father Williams in his foreword has thanked Nigel Kerry for the Musical events in the Centenary and I would like to add my own personal thanks to Nigel who kept his head whilst all others were losing theirs ... including me!

T.V.M.